AGENCIES AND FOSTER CHILDREN

DEBORAH SHAPIRO

It is an undisputed if troubling fact of modern city life that the contemporary urban family is under severe strain and requires the support of other social institutions. What is in dispute, however, is the effectiveness of those institutions—in particular, the foster care system—which have been developed to help these families cope with the overwhelming burdens of poverty and deprivation.

AGENCIES AND FOSTER CHILDREN is the most systematic picture available on the part that agencies play in our foster care system. The book reports upon that portion of an impressive five-year study of the foster care system in New York City which focused upon the functioning of the agencies and their child care workers. For this study over 600 children placed in foster care were followed from the time of placement, and data were obtained on the attitudes of the child care workers toward the families and children they served. A special substudy on the workers demonstrates how their attitudes influenced the outcome of place-

ment and makes a comparison of workers in public and voluntary agencies.

More than just a presentation and analysis of data, however, this important study tests some of the basic assumptions of casework. The findings indicate that despite strong professions of concern for reuniting families the network of foster care agencies tends to contribute toward their continuing in R CHILDREN foster care. They suggest further that widely reported developments in the field—such as subsidies, relaxed standards, preference to foster parents, single parent adoption, and interracial adoption—make progress appear to be more advanced than is the case. In conclusion the study discusses structural and ideological impediments to change in the foster care system and methods for overcoming them.

This is an indispensable book for all child welfare researchers and foster care agencies and personnel.

**SOCIAL WORK
AND SOCIAL ISSUES,
COLUMBIA UNIVERSITY
SCHOOL OF SOCIAL WORK**

ial Issues
of Social Work

Deborah Shapiro is a research associate with the Child Welfare League of America. She has had extensive experience as a caseworker and has been involved in research in the areas of maternal and child health, mental retardation, illegitimacy, and adoption, as well as in foster care.

Deborah Shapiro

AGENCIES
AND
FOSTER
CHILDREN

COLUMBIA UNIVERSITY PRESS

NEW YORK   1976

LIBRARY OF CONGRESS CATALOGING IN PUBLICATION DATA

Shapiro, Deborah.
  Agencies and children.
  Includes bibliographical references and index.
  1. Foster home care—New York (City)—
Longitudinal studies. I. Title.
HV875.S47   362.7'33'097471   75-40052
          ISBN 0-231-03578-0

COLUMBIA UNIVERSITY PRESS

NEW YORK   GUILDFORD, SURREY

For Sharon Sarah

===

*my own
private expert
on children*

The Columbia University School of Social Work publication series, "Social Work and Social Issues," is concerned with the implications of social work practice and social welfare policy for solving problems. Each volume is an independent work. The series is intended to contribute to the knowledge base of social work education, to facilitate communication with related disciplines, and to serve as a background for public policy discussion. Other books in the series are

Shirley Jenkins, *editor*
Social Security in International Perspective 1969

George Brager and Harry Specht
Community Organizing 1973

Alfred J. Kahn, *editor*
Shaping the New Social Work 1973

Shirley Jenkins and Elaine Norman
Beyond Placement: Mothers View Foster Care 1975

FOREWORD

ON JANUARY 1, 1966, John V. Lindsay assumed office as the Mayor of the City of New York. On the very same day, the city's transit workers went on strike and much of the normal life of the metropolis was paralyzed. In the midst of this turmoil, a phenomenon commanding less public attention was also launched: the start of a longitudinal investigation of foster children. Any child who entered foster care in New York City as a public charge on that New Year's Day and over the following eight months, and who had never been in care before, became a likely candidate for inclusion in the study.

While the transit strike hampered the operations of the staff of the public welfare agency sufficiently to require them to postpone having the project's case readers perform case finding and content analysis activity in their midst, this problem was soon overcome—as were a host of other difficulties, large and small—that can beset extended studies in real-life situations.

Longitudinal investigations enjoy high status among child development researchers as the preferred design for studying developmental changes. Such studies, however, are expensive to mount and extraordinarily difficult to carry out. Thus, longitudinal investigations in child development have been relatively few and far between. A small number of classic studies stand as monuments to the persistence and stubborn commitment of a small band of stalwart investigators.

Longitudinal studies of foster children have been in even shorter supply. In fact, it would appear from a search of the literature that they have been nonexistent. When the Columbia University School of Social Work was given the opportunity to promulgate a large-scale programmatic investigation under a newly authorized federal program, the Child Welfare Research and Demonstration Grants Program, we proposed undertaking a five-year longitudinal study of a large sample of foster children. Such an endeavor seemed badly needed. Previous studies reporting on the effects upon children of maternal deprivation and exposure to foster care arrangements had excited public interest because of their provocative findings about the dire consequences of such experiences. However many of these studies were suspect because they were based upon very small samples, were retrospective rather than prospective, utilized one-shot assessments rather than repeated assessments, and were narrow gauged; they measured only a single aspect of the child's development—e.g., intelligence, proneness to delinquency, or a personality trait. The award of a substantial federal grant made it possible to carry out research without these limitations.

The reader should be aware that Columbia University Press is publishing three related volumes dealing with the foster care phenomenon in longitudinal perspective. This volume and a second one (David Fanshel and Eugene B. Shinn, *Children in Foster Care: A Longitudinal Investigation*) are based upon grants awarded to the Child Welfare Research Program at the Columbia University School of Social Work. They deal with the same sample of cases. Shapiro focuses upon the nature of agency services to the children and families, while Fanshel and Shinn concentrate on how the children fared over the five-year period of investigation. A parallel research effort—the Family Welfare Research Program under the direction of Dr. Shirley Jenkins—was focused on the parents of the child subjects and resulted in the volume *Beyond Placement: Mothers View Foster Care*, co-authored with Dr. Elaine Norman. We thus have the unusual circumstance of a longitudinal study of foster children, their parents, and the agencies serving them carried out as parallel investigations. We therefore see the foster care phenomenon from the perspective of the three key actors.

My relationship with Deborah Shapiro began when she was a doctoral candidate in a course I taught in the early 1960s. For a whole semester she sat silent, obviously attentive, but choosing not to say a word as her more voluble colleagues held forth without reticence. I had begun to think that the silence reflected a disinterest in the issues being discussed or perhaps even a dullness in her personality. However, I changed my opinion when I read her final paper. In it she analyzed in considerable depth the strengths and shortcomings of two major empirical studies recently reported in the sociological literature. Her criticisms were incisive and reflected an agile mind at work. In addition, her classroom behavior left me unprepared for the sharp wit and emotional force in her writing.

Some years later I was looking for a study director to head the agency phase of the Child Welfare Research Program's longitudinal study of foster children, and was delighted to find that Dr. Shapiro was available for this challenging undertaking. Thus began an association between us of some nine years duration. The nature of this relationship is difficult to describe in simple terms. Often, Dr. Shapiro chose to introduce me to newcomers as her "boss." I would always smile inwardly at such moments because I had learned over time that she was hardly one to be *bossed*; and such an approach would have been absolutely wrong in her case. It would be more accurate to describe our relationship as collegial, based upon mutual respect and friendship.

I set out at an early stage the broad general outlines of Dr. Shapiro's enterprise and she took it up from there, fashioning her research based upon conceptions and approaches that came out of her own cognitive grasp of what was required. In the course of our separate parallel ventures—I in the child description effort and she in analyzing the nature and consequence of agency service investments—we influenced each other in a variety of ways. I am clearly beholden to her for a number of important measures used in analyzing the influences of the foster care experience upon the children as revealed in the companion volume. However, it is important to identify Dr. Shapiro's book as essentially reflecting her own product, the result of a prodigious investment of her time and creative energy over many years.

The herculean nature of the author's achievement in writing this volume can be partially appreciated by some simple data. In the first year of the study, Dr. Shapiro's interviewing staff completed 858 telephone interviews obtained from 511 workers, covering 98 percent of the study sample. Over the four cycles of interviewing conducted during a five-year period, 2,274 interviews were completed with 1,107 workers dispersed among 84 agencies. There were only two occasions during the four cycles

where workers refused to cooperate with her staff. Her study lends support
for the use of the telephone interview as a most suitable vehicle for large-
scale field interviewing.

Dr. Shapiro's findings are bound to arouse interest among those who
have long viewed with misgiving the fact that so many children seem
"adrift" in foster care. There has been pressure applied upon child welfare agencies to *do something* about the plight of these children. Her findings suggest that there can indeed be a positive payoff when agency service time is invested in families. She comments: "The fact that service
assets do make a difference within the first two years indicates that agency
effort does result in a different, usually a better picture of the family
which leads to discharge. By implication, an increase in investment
could result in earlier discharges with a reduction in damage for the
child, the family, and the public as taxpayers." Yet, disquiet is also
created by the author's finding that the degree of support given families
by agencies appears time-limited: "The supportive function is fulfilled, if
at all, only for about two years after the crisis that precipitates placement.
After this, the agency becomes in effect a custodian for the child and, as
earlier studies have shown, the family is increasingly alienated."

Here, one will find not only the first in-depth view of the role of
agency investment in the foster care drama, but will also gain a perspective from a substudy in which interviews were conducted with 223 social
workers who carried case responsibilities in serving the children and families studied. Dr. Shapiro illuminates the kinds of pressures experienced
by workers in the voluntary and public agency sectors, the forces interfer-
ing with their ability to serve their clients, and their orientation toward
continuing employment in child welfare. This spinoff study complements
the research into agency investment, and together these two pieces of
scholarship tell us more than has hitherto been available about the
strengths and weaknesses of the service system to which so many children
and families are exposed.

This volume should provoke a close examination of the systems we
have created to serve the needs of children requiring care away from
home. It should lead to a more rational deployment of precious staff
resources in order to offer the children a maximum opportunity to be returned to their own families early in their placement experience. The
volume should also provide a frame of reference for future studies of
child welfare agencies and their service programs. Its publication was

made possible by the remarkable cooperation of 84 agencies, a mark of their willingness to have their own performance carefully scrutinized. Such receptivity to research bodes well for the future health of the system.

David Fanshel
Director, Child Welfare Research Program,
Columbia University School of Social Work
February 1976

ACKNOWLEDGMENTS

AS EVERYONE FAMILIAR WITH THE FIELD KNOWS, research reports have long since ceased to be the products of an individual enterprise involving a scholar with a clipboard and a typewriter. This study, like those of similar scope and magnitude, is the result of the collective efforts of many people. The study director assumes responsibility, along with the principal investigator, for the quality of the effort and, in presenting the report for publication, has the pleasure of acknowledging a long list of debts. For this phase of the Child Welfare Research Program, major credit belongs to the following people:

Geraldine Simpson, Sonia Austrian, and Carol Hasto for supervision of a complex field operation on the main study, followed by equally complex coding procedures.

Louise Elbaum and William Meezan, who did the same job with the same high level of competence for the substudy reported in part III.

Tobi Weissberger for attending to the endless clerical work a study of this scope entails.

Barbara Sutton, Elizabeth Connolly, Irene Blum, and Eva Russo, who stood out in an excellent group of interviewers and stayed with the study through several cycles of data collection.

Carol Martin, Varda Brahms, and Jayne Sherman, who performed exceptionally well through several cycles of coding.

Sumitra Mohan and Carlos Stecher, who dealt with mountains of IBM cards and computer output, helping to solve many analytic problems.

Ann Gerloch for her meticulous secretarial work and exemplary manuscript typing.

John Grundy for his knowledge of statistics, understanding of computer programs, and general patience with a non–statistically minded study director.

Shirley Jenkins, Elaine Norman, and Eugene Shinn for a high level of professionalism as colleagues.

David Fanshel, the most benign and supportive of project directors.

Trudy Festinger of the New York University School of Social Work, who read the manuscript with painstaking care and gave me the benefits of her great acuity.

This study was financed by Grant No. SRS–89–P–80050–209, originally from the Children's Bureau and later from the Community Services Administration, Social and Rehabilitation Services, of the United States Department of Health, Education, and Welfare. For this, we are, together with our colleagues, profoundly appreciative of the initiative, foresight, and understanding of the research field demonstrated to us repeatedly by Dr. Charles Gershenson of the Research and Evaluation Division of the Office of Child Development.

Deborah Shapiro
February 1976

CONTENTS

AGENCIES AND FOSTER CHILDREN

Social Work and Social Issues
Columbia University School of Social Work

chapter one

DESIGN OF THE STUDY

IT IS WELL-DOCUMENTED that the family in contemporary urban society is under severe strain and in need of support from other social institutions. Among the variety of supporting institutions which have been developed in this country during the last century are those which provide children with complete care away from home whenever the family can no longer fulfill its normal childrearing function. Over 350,000 children were cared for in this manner in the United States in 1971.[1] In New York City, over 28,000 children were in foster care in 1973.[2] Many of them will spend their entire childhood supported either by tax money or voluntary philanthropies or a combination of the two; some will eventually return to their original families or to a family reconstituted by a parent's remarriage, live with a relative willing to assume responsibility or, occasionally, find an adoptive home.

Nineteenth-century foster care agencies regarded a child's placement away from home as permanent, but during the last half century, with the development of social work as a profession, agencies providing placement have come to set a high value on the reunion of children with their families and profess to support the natural family unit. Whether such agencies actually work toward the reunification of families is a much discussed

---

1. National Center for Social Statistics, U.S. Department of Health, Education, and Welfare, *Children Served by Public Welfare Agencies and Voluntary Child Welfare Agencies and Institutions, March, 1971* (Washington, D.C.: DHEW Publication No. [SS] 73–03258, Table 8, April 27, 1973).
2. Community Council of Greater New York, Research and Program Planning Information, "Trends in Foster Care in New York City," 1960–1973, *Research Notes*, No. 12, March 1, 1974.

question in the child welfare field. Whatever the facts are, agencies do have a clientele of children and families to whom they are at least nominally committed to help function as normal families. Wherever the achievement of this goal is impossible, the agency has an alternative commitment to provide a substitute form of childrearing that will produce as nearly "normal" an adult as might have been produced by a natural family.

The achievement of these goals (or the failure to achieve them) is not necessarily the direct consequence of an agency program. A child may return to his family largely because its members had strengths or resources of their own or because conditions in the community changed for the better. Similarly, a child may improve emotionally while in foster care, not because of any special quality in the service given him, but because of his own healthy adaptive capacities. On the other hand, some families are so broken by events as to resist the best of available social services and some children are so damaged by their previous experiences that the warmest of foster homes has little effect. In such cases, the agency plays a relatively passive "holding" role, aimed at preventing further deterioration.

In most instances, however, social agencies make the eminently reasonable assumption that the quantity and quality of their services are an important contributing factor in whatever improvements occur in the children and families they serve. Justifying this assumption with tangible evidence that the improvements are indeed associated with professional service is by no means simple. Agency executives find a variety of indications of achievement—stable placements, long service records of foster parents, academic and other successes of children, etc.—but harassed workers confronted daily with unhappy children, demanding or irresponsible natural parents, angry institutional counselors, confused or anxious foster parents, still ask the plaintive question, "Do we really do any good?"

At face value, the answer to such a question is "yes." On the strength of sheer statistical probability, a system of agency services to which thousands of children are exposed undoubtedly does some of them some "good" at some time. The truly perplexing problems are the assessment of how much "good" is done, understanding the nature of the "good," and knowing the conditions under which "good" work is carried out.

Early in the planning phase of the Child Welfare Research Program's longitudinal study of 624 children in care, a decision was made to include in the study design data that reflected the perspectives of the principal participants. The children, the family, and the agencies were each to be examined directly; the children with psychological examinations and descriptive data provided by those in a position to observe them, the natural parents with field interviews, and the agencies with an instrument addressed to the social workers assigned to each child or family. The intent was to avoid one of the limitations characteristic of survey research, namely the tendency to focus on a single role within a given social system, thus limiting the conclusions to those which can be based on data obtained from that source. Studies involving data provided by social workers often raise the question as to how different the findings might have been had the clients been interviewed directly. Data based on clients' views often raise the question as to how their workers perceive the same issues. This latter limitation is particularly pertinent in research in the social work profession, whose practitioner-consumers are primarily concerned with the application of research findings. A study in which a description of the problems of natural parents or of foster parents is obtained only from the subjects themselves would give little information, except by inference, as to which of these problems could be modified by social workers, and would not answer the practitioner's proverbial complaint, "but we *know* all that; the problem is what are we *doing* about it?"

The Exploratory Phase

The directive to develop the agency phase of the study led to an exploratory review of the child welfare literature, which was focused on two basic questions: To what kinds of outcomes or end results does foster care lead? What factors in the agency system are most likely to influence such outcomes? Reflections on these questions led to a working paper which served as a basis for staff discussion which, in turn, led to a definition of the study's central concept being concerned with the agency "investment"—or the extent of the agency's commitment to its foster care clients.

It was noted that "outcome" could be defined at two different levels: the client's (the child and his family) and the staff's. The outcome of foster care for child and family could be: (1) A long period of placement (more than three months, less than total childhood), terminating in return home; [3] (2) a long period of placement, terminating in adoption; (3) placement for duration of childhood with minimal change; (4) repeated placements for the duration of childhood.

In terms of the values of the child welfare system, the first category represents the most desirable outcome, the last the least desirable, while the second and third lie between the two extremes. Outcomes for the staff, such as employment stability and satisfactory work performance, were also identified, but since the study was focused on the sample of children, the first class of outcomes remained the more relevant for the main study. [4]

The review of the child welfare and social science literature, as well as some of the data collected in a preliminary study of executives, [5] helped to identify a number of variables which had a potential for influencing outcome. Staff discussion of the paper led to a decision that the study would focus on the agency's investment in the children in the main study. This approach had the major advantage of insuring that data from the agency study could be systematically related to data from other phases of the study. Worker knowledge of the children, for instance, could be related to the results of psychological testing. [6] On the other hand, this decision meant limiting the agency variables to those which were associated with the handling of individual cases and about which workers were knowledgeable. In general, it was felt that the advantages of this approach outweighed the disadvantages and the study then moved from its theory-oriented exploratory phase to facing some of the realities of data collection in an extremely complex, heavily pressured, and understaffed social agency system.

The process of putting the concept of "investment" in operation was accompanied by a period of field observation in four of the cooperating agencies, selected to reflect the diversity of services given in New York. Two offered long-term foster home care, another institutional care for disturbed children, and the fourth was a multifunction agency offering

3. Short-term periods of placement were eliminated by the sampling decision, which limited the study to children in care three months or longer.
4. Staff outcomes later become the focus of an ancillary study reported in part III.
5. Reported in Frances Kroll, "Perspectives on Foster Care in New York City," Center for Research and Demonstration, mimeographed, (New York: Columbia University School of Social Work, 1967).
6. Data relating workers' information and test results is reported in David Fanshel and Eugene Shinn, *Children in Foster Care* (New York: Columbia University Press, forthcoming).

both institutional and foster home care on a temporary or long-term basis. Observation consisted primarily of attendance at sessions with psychiatrists and at interagency discussions, which were focused primarily on the problems of the early phases of placement. There were 15 such meetings, attended by the study director and the research assistant assigned to the agency phase. Informal discussions with supervisors and workers also added to the fund of knowledge which in turn helped to create viable instruments. Two of the agencies involved later supplied respondents to enable the staff to pretest the questionnaire and the interview schedule that were developed from this experience.

Development of Instruments

In the study, and in this book, "investment" means literally "what is put in." Occasionally, it was used interchangeably with computer-age terms such as "input" and even the standard English "contribution." In putting this concept into use, we realized that the design of the study limited the description of "investment" to the work done with individual children and their families. The agency's investment in such collective matters as clothing allowances, recreational facilities, medical care, board rates for foster parents, etc., would be almost impossible to assess through a study of children widely scattered among different agencies. For example, three or four study children assigned to a given agency might have no need for a remedial reading program, even though such a program may have represented a considerable investment of time and effort on the part of the agency staff. It was necessary to assume that all agencies provided the children in their care with maintenance, medical attention, recreation, and schooling as required by the state licensing laws. The adequacy of any of these basic services might vary considerably, but assessments of quality would be difficult to infer from a sample of children chosen to meet the requirements of a developmental study. When taking these considerations into account, we defined "investment" as the effort and skill contributed by the agency staff in helping a sample of children and their families, over and above the basic requirements of maintenance.

The concept of investment was then developed into a series of measures, data for which could be obtained from the agency workers. The first and most self-evident measure was time and effort: How much time did each worker spend on the study subject in the form of interviews, discussions with other agencies, supervisory conferences, psychiatric consultation, etc.? We knew that we could not expect a precise time-and-motion breakdown of worker activity, but assuming that a reasonably complete account could be obtained from most workers, major activities, such as interviews and home visits, and secondary activities such as telephone calls could be estimated with reasonable accuracy. Errors based on worker recall or incomplete recording were likely to be common, but it would still be possible to distinguish among those children who received a relatively high investment of worker time and effort, those for whom worker "input" was average, and those for whom it was minimal.

Investment could also be measured in terms of the worker's training and professional experience, items which reflect the financial investment of the agency since they are directly related to salary levels.

These two measures of investment provided the core of "hard" data, since they are relatively factual and not subject to so much distortion as measures consisting mainly of attitudinal statements and evaluative judgments. Despite the measurement problems involved in using subjective judgments as data, the qualitative aspects of agency investment could not be ignored. The possibility that such factors as a worker's identification with a child or her relationship with the mother might be far more potent in determining the outcome for that child than the worker's training or the number of interviews she had done had to be taken into consideration. In the final version of the instrument used, the workers were asked for detailed descriptions of the child and the family, in which the primary aim was to enable the research staff to make judgments as to how knowledgeable the worker was about the case and to what extent she was identified with or interested in the study subject and his family. The plan of the study precluded extensive pretesting and refinement of measures, making it necessary to settle for gross judgments in which a measure of confidence could be placed because they were made by trained and experienced staff.

In addition to staff judgments of workers' knowledge and attitudes, questions that measured workers' judgments of the quality of care were introduced into the instruments. These included information about the experience of foster parents, and institutional staff. Workers were also asked for an account of the placement process, and of their relations with other agencies, in order to assess the extent to which the child's course in placement was facilitated by interagency cooperation or hampered by bureaucratic entanglements.

Since her training and experience alone did not reflect the worker's ability to invest as much as might be desired in any given child or family, it was also necessary to introduce a series of measures which reflected the atmosphere in which the worker functioned, specifically the degree of pressure she was under to give service. These included such factual items as size of caseload, but also consisted of more subjective evaluations, such as the amount of time spent in administrative tasks as compared to direct contact with clients, whether workers felt themselves to be under pressure, and to what extent they derived satisfaction from their work.

With these as basic areas of agency investment, other items were added to the instrument to serve other purposes such as facilitating comparison with other phases of the study and to assist in the complicated task of following the sample for five years.

Instruments

We first assumed that the appropriate instrument for the study's purposes would be a questionnaire; it seemed appropriate because agency workers met the usual criteria for questionnaire respondents (literacy and motivation) and because it is usually the least costly of instruments. Experience, however, soon demonstrated that a questionnaire was dysfunctional in several respects. Since the sample covered many children in diverse situations, the number of subschedules necessary to meet various contingencies was high, making the schedule inordinately lengthy. A pretest indicated that a respondent filling out a questionnaire took twice as long as an interview covering the same subject, since in the latter case the interviewer automatically eliminated irrelevant topics. It also seemed likely that workers would resist any lengthy schedule, as they were already doing so with the forms required by their own work, as well as those required by other phases of the study; the resistance would be reinforced by an occupational distaste for the "pigeonholing" of clients required by the precoded categories characteristic of questionnaires.

Telephone interviewing was suggested by the experience of another study [7] which had succeeded in obtaining a high response rate from physicians. We noted that the use of the phone did not bias the sample,

7. John Colombotos, "The Effects of Personal vs. Telephone Interviews on Socially Acceptable Response" (Paper presented at the annual meeting of the American Association for Public Opinion Research, Groton, Connecticut, May 14, 1965).

since all workers could be reached. Telephone discussions of client problems are a normal routine in most agencies and thus would not introduce an unfamiliar situation or another form to be filled out. A small pretest, divided evenly between respondents who filled out a questionnaire and those who were interviewed on the phone, confirmed the impression that the telephone interview was less time consuming, and produced less resistance among respondents.[8] Although obviously more expensive than a questionnaire, the telephone interview was less of a budgetary problem than conventional in-person interviewing, especially for a study that already required a separate field operation to reach natural parents.[9]

An exception to the telephone interviews was made for one agency which maintained that its telephone lines were too limited to permit extended conversations. Occasionally other in-person interviewing was done at the request of an agency. Case readings were sometimes substituted for or used to supplement interviews, usually when the worker assigned had left and supervisors were unable to find a suitable alternate respondent. This was particularly necessary during the second cycle of data collection, when a department in the public agency was closed and its workers transferred. The amount of data collected by such deviations from the established procedure was relatively small and there was no evidence of significant effects on the findings.

Data Collection

Data concerning the study children and their workers were collected at four different times. The first series of interviews was called Time 1, and was conducted in 1966–67. There were 858 interviews with 511 workers; the interviews covered 616 children (98 percent of the study sample of

8. Colombotos did some experiments which indicated little significant difference in the extent to which telephone interviews elicit socially acceptable or stereotyped responses when compared to in-person interviews. After the study was planned, telephone interviewing was successfully used in other research projects, such as that of Derek Phillips and Kevin Clancy, reported in "Response Biases in Field Studies of Mental Illness," *American Sociological Review* 35, no. 31 (June 1970): 503–15, as well as in Trudy Festinger's *Why Some Choose Not to Adopt Through Agencies* (New York: Metropolitan Applied Research Center, Inc. 1972), p. 25.
9. Shirley Jenkins and Elaine Norman, *Filial Deprivation and Maternal Care* (New York: Columbia University Press, 1972).

624 children).[10] This interview occurred when most children had been in placement between six and nine months. The second series (Time 2) was conducted one year later. This time there were 656 interviews with 363 workers; the interviews covered 493 children (79 percent of the original sample) who had received some form of agency service during this period.[11]

The third series of interviews (Time 3) was conducted in 1969–70, usually around the third anniversary of the original interview.[12] This series required 445 interviews with 352 workers; the interviews covered 396 children (62 percent of the original sample). The final series (Time 4) was conducted in 1970–71. It required 315 interviews with 231 workers; the interviews covered 275 children (44 percent of the original sample).[13] Each series involved interviews with workers who had participated earlier and with workers new to the study; the latter outnumbered the former each time. Altogether, 1,107 workers were required to give 2,274 interviews in order to obtain a reasonably complete picture of agency investment in the study children over the period covered.

Interviews could not be limited to one per child in each cycle for several reasons, principally because intake responsibility in New York City usually rested with workers at the Bureau of Child Welfare or with a probation officer of the Family Court. Physical care of the children is provided by city shelters and temporary boarding home facilities, as well as the nurseries of two large Catholic agencies which accept infants and toddlers for temporary care on a nonsectarian basis. For this study, an interview with an intake agency worker for data about the family was needed as well as one with the worker of a child-caring agency to obtain data about the child. At Time 1, a second interview was completed for 42

10. Eight study children had been placed for adoption by the time their workers were contacted by study staff and their records were not available.
11. Interviews took place as long as the agency continued to give service. The number of children about whom data were obtained at each point in time includes those in aftercare or discharged during the time period covered and is always larger than the number of children who were still in foster care at each point in time.
12. When the study staff was notified that a child had been discharged, the interview was scheduled for the earliest possible date to avoid the problem of "stale" or unobtainable data, which would have resulted had the anniversary schedule been strictly interpreted.
13. The reduction in the number of sample children covered in each series was almost entirely due to the cessation of agency activity. Four administrative errors resulting in failure to assign an interviewer and two refusals were the only other reasons for not obtaining data.

percent of the children. The need for double interviewing diminished with each series, as the care of the children was taken over by a single agency offering long-term care, but it never entirely disappeared since several agencies followed the practice of assigning the family and the child to different workers. Fourteen percent of the study children required second interviews at Time 2 and twelve percent at Time 3, but only five percent at Time 4.

During the five years in which data were collected, 23 interviewers were employed, seven of whom remained for more than one cycle of data collection. Their efforts were supplemented by the three research assistants under whose supervision they worked, as well as two case readers and eleven graduate students who were taking a course in research methods.

Since the assignment of the study children followed the agency's normal procedures, it was possible for workers to have more than one study child in their case loads. At Time 1, 40 percent of the workers were interviewed more than once. Multiple interviewing was particularly characteristic of the workers in the overcrowded city shelters, one of whom had to be interviewed no less than 14 times. As children were transferred into the care of the voluntary agencies, which form the larger part of the New York City network and which are generally better staffed than the city agencies, the need for multiple interviews was reduced to 18 percent of the respondents at Time 2 and remained at that level for each of the remaining cycles.

In general, most workers proved to be satisfactory respondents who answered most questions fully and thoughtfully, showed concern about their clients, and expressed themselves frankly about many professional problems. However, there undeniably were those who were self-conscious, evasive, or prone to giving stereotyped responses. At Time 1, 21 percent of the respondents were categorized as presenting some type of interviewing problem; another 5 percent were considered so limited as to cast doubts on the validity of the data they gave. At Time 2, the proportion of "problem" respondents declined to 18 percent, to 10 percent at Time 3, and rose again to 17 percent at Time 4.

At Time 1, when problems with data collection were greatest, the difficulties tended to stem from the fact that the public agencies controlling the intake procedures were also prone to high turnover and low levels of training. Most workers were young, new to their jobs, and worked under

heavy pressure. Thus a research interview, which required the demonstration of at least a minimal degree of knowledge about a case and some
indication that something was being "done," put some of the workers on
the defensive, occasionally to the point of open hostility. Contrary to the
usual practice in research interviewing, interviewers were instructed to
avoid excessive probing. Experience indicated that the respondents were
evasive principally because they were embarrassed by their lack of knowledge and were reluctant to admit their ignorance. This problem diminished considerably in the later phases of the study, reflecting the greater
training and experience of the later respondents. The principal problems
of the later cycles were the workers' periodic eruptions over the time
required by the study, particularly if they were expected to respond to
more than one instrument of the inquiry within a short time. The workers nearly always ventilated their feelings, however, and gave adequate interviews in spite of their resentment.

The problem of contamination was another source of concern in data
collection. The identity of the study children could not be concealed
from the workers, nor could the fact that the children selected represented only a very small proportion of each agency's caseload; therefore,
it was possible for agencies, if they were so inclined, to treat the study
subjects differently from other children in the interests of making a better
impression.

Evidence that handling had been influenced by the fact that the respondent was a study subject was recorded whenever it came to the interviewer's attention. The final analysis showed some form of contamination
or suspicion of it for five percent of the children—or 33 cases—over the
full course of the study. Of these, more than half were cases in which
there was an apparent increase in some form of activity—contacts with
other agencies, visits to the child or its family—usually between the time
the worker telephoned for an appointment and the time the interview
took place. This increase apparently occurred because the worker wanted
to be certain she could demonstrate knowledge of the case to the interviewer. Most of these activities did not appear to affect the basic decisions
made in each case. In general, some degree of contamination is probably
unavoidable in a study such as this, but it also seems likely that difficult
working conditions operated, in this instance, in favor of the study. The
pressures under which workers acted made it unlikely that many significant decisions were influenced by the child's involvement in the study.

Whatever took place in the course of these experience in foster care probably would have taken place had the child not been in the study at all.

Data Analysis

Data analysis followed standard research procedures: code books were developed, coders were trained, coding decisions were punched on IBM cards. Harvard Data-Text programs for the IBM 360 were used to carry out the analyses desired. A 10 percent reliability check on coding decisions was completed for each cycle of data. Whenever there was more than one interview about a child, a decision was made at each time cycle as to which interview contained better data about the child, about the family, and about the agency service. An interview was presumed to be "better" if the worker had first-hand knowledge of the child or the family, knew them longer, and gave more detailed information than the other worker on the case. In analyses requiring an unduplicated count, only the interview containing better data in the relevant area was used. This procedure also minimized the effects of the Time 1 data collection problems, since much of the weaker data did not need to be used.

Once the data was coded and checked for errors, indices were developed of various types of agency investment by computing the Pearson r for all combinations of variables which formed clusters of items considered to be logical reflections of different types of investment.[14] This step was repeated for each phase of data collection, using variables comparable in content to those which formed indices at Time 1. With some modifications, most of these indices could be used for the purpose of describing changes over time. Single variables were also used for purposes of comparison where no index could be developed.

All the investment measures were cross-tabulated against three forms of outcome: the status of the child with respect to continuation in care, the worker's perception of improvement in the child, and her perception of improvement in the family. The variables having statistically significant relationships to each outcome were entered in a regression analysis together with variables describing the client and the agency system, to determine whether the investment variables remained influential when other factors were controlled. Content analyses of deviant cases were also

14. The contents of those indices, which were significantly related to outcome, are described in chapters 6 and 7.

done whenever there were indications that the experiences of small sub-samples were substantively significant or were likely to throw light on some of the more puzzling relationships described.

Part I gives the reader an overview of the workers who participated in the study, the placement problems as they saw them, and a picture of the children and the families as reported by the workers. Part II takes up in detail the relationship between various types of agency investment and their effects on the children and the family, as well other variables which had a significant impact. Part III describes a substudy of child welfare workers and presents findings about the impact of their work experience on their careers as well as on the clients in the study. The final chapter will summarize the key findings and discuss their implications for the field.

PART ONE

THE STUDY POPULATION

chapter two

AGENCIES AND WORKERS

T O PLACE THE FINDINGS on the impact of agency investment in the New York City child welfare system in some perspective, a description of the study samples—workers, families, and children—is presented in this and the succeeding chapters in part I. First to be described are the agencies and the workers from whom the data on the study children and their families were obtained, since both their qualifications and limitations have to be kept in mind in evaluating the data. Chapter 3 will describe the family sample as seen by the workers while chapter 4 will describe the children. Chapter 5 will present data on key aspects of the placement situation.

The purpose of these chapters is to present a broad overview of the characteristics of the principal actors represented in the agency network. Limited time and space preclude a detailed discussion of the problems reflected in the figures given. Each topic represents a major problem in the child welfare field worthy of detailed analysis and discussion on its own merits, which the knowledgeable reader may miss. For our purposes here, these chapters represent a backdrop for the specific findings of later chapters.

Agencies Represented

Of the 87 agencies eligible for the study,[1] only 3 drew no study subjects during the five-year period the children were in placement and therefore

1. Large departments of the public agency and of the larger multifunction agencies were counted as separate units.

had no workers in the sample. Thus, the total worker sample of 1,074 was widely dispersed among 84 agencies.[2] The largest group (111 workers) employed in a single agency were those serving the intake department of the Bureau of Child Welfare, but even this group constitutes only 10 percent of the total worker sample. Only 9 agencies were represented by over thirty workers while 48 were represented by seven or fewer. The number of agencies also varied with each time cycle, ranging from 64 at Time 1 to 42 at the final cycle, when two-thirds of the children in the sample had been discharged.

For the entire period, 68 percent of the workers represented voluntary agencies while 32 percent represented public agencies. At Time 1, the worker sample was almost evenly divided between those representing public agencies (49 percent) and those representing voluntary agencies (51 percent). With the second cycle, only 23 percent of the workers new to the study represented public agencies. Among those from voluntary agencies, 48 percent represented Catholic agencies, 17 percent Protestant, 6 percent Jewish, and 6 percent nonsectarian. Of the voluntary agency sample, 43 percent worked in agencies serving fewer than 150 children, 24 percent in agencies serving from 150 to 300 children at a time, and 33 percent in agencies serving over 300 children.

Of the entire sample, workers assigned to children in long-term foster homes constituted the largest group (37 percent) but the proportion representing long-term institutional care was almost as great (33 percent). The remaining 30 percent were workers assigned to temporary services. Over the four time cycles, the proportion of workers in foster home services rose from 19 percent at Time 1 to 51 percent at Time 4, while the proportion representing long-term institutions remained relatively stable. The group representing shelter services obviously declined sharply after the first year.

It should not be assumed that the worker sample represents all or even most of the workers who served the study children and their families. As will be seen later, 40 percent of the children had experienced worker turnover by the time of the first interview and more than 50 percent experienced turnover at each of the subsequent cycles. Cumulative figures indicate that children who continued in agency care at Time 2 had a me-

2. A detailed description of the New York City system is available in Eugene B. Shinn, "The New York City System of Foster Care," mimeographed (New York: Columbia University School of Social Work, 1968). Dr. Shinn was a Study Director of the School's Child Welfare Research Program.

dian of 6 workers, in direct contact with them and their families, with a range as high as 12. For children continuing in care through Time 3, the median was 7 with a range as high as 16. For those children who were in care throughout the five-year time span of the study, the median number of workers was 9 with a range that reached 17. In all, approximately 2,500 workers [3] served the 616 children in the agency study, or more than twice as many as were interviewed.

The Workers

Demographic characteristics

The workers were predominantly young, white, female, and single; 76 percent were women while 69 percent were under 30. The predominance of the youngest group—those under 25—declined somewhat from 45 percent at Time 1 to 37 percent at Time 4, but still remained the largest proportion. Of the workers sampled, 76 percent were white while 15 percent were black and the remainder of Hispanic, Oriental, or mixed origins, proportions which did not vary significantly over the time span involved. Of the total sample 60 percent were single, 35 percent married, and the remaining 5 percent formerly married. Since the group at Time 1 was younger, it was also more likely to be single than those who came into the study later. Twenty-one percent of the workers had children, a proportion that was stable for the period of the study.

Job titles, training, and experience

A large majority of the respondents had the title of "caseworker," even though relatively few had been formally trained as such. Other titles were case aide, probation officer, senior case worker, supervisor, field work student, psychologist, and psychiatrist.

For the entire sample, 46 percent had only a bachelor's degree, while 22 percent had a master's degree in social work. [4] The remaining 32 per-

---

3. A precise figure cannot be given since the number of duplications among workers not interviewed is not ascertainable.

4. Precise figures which reflect the degree of professionalization in social work are difficult to obtain. Arnulf Pins ("The Number, Size, Output, and Programs of Schools of Social Work and the Need for Professional Manpower," in *Social Work Education and Social Welfare Manpower* [New York: Council on Social Work Education, 1965]), estimated that of 116,000 social welfare positions, about 80 percent are filled by people who do not have graduate professional education. Thus, the proportion of trained staff in the study sample is similar to what it is for the country and the profession as a whole.

cent had some graduate training but had not achieved the degree. The first-year sample of workers has an even lower proportion of trained workers—17 percent—but it increased sharply to 31 percent at Time 2, when most of the children had entered the care of voluntary agencies, and reached 35 percent at the final cycle.

Another indicator of the professional level of the sample is the fact that 37 percent of the workers had no plans to obtain professional training at the time they were interviewed. The proportion of workers not oriented toward a degree was relatively high at Time 1 (40 percent) but dropped to 26 percent at Time 2 and stayed at that level for the remainder of the study. The change is probably attributable to the shift to the voluntary system, where emphasis on training is stronger.

In keeping with their youth and relatively low level of training, 56 percent of the workers had been with the agencies they represented for a year or less. For 58 percent, employment with the agency they represented was their only experience in the field of social work. The median total experience for the sample was two years. The experience level was particularly low for the first two cycles but increased for the later cycles; the inexperienced constituted 64 percent of the Time 2 sample but only 35 percent at Time 4. Again this is probably due to the shift to the voluntary system.

Of the total sample, 19 percent defined their responsibility in terms of such agency procedures as intake. The balance was about evenly divided among those responsible for the child and the child-caring person—either foster parents or institutional counselors (21 percent of the sample)—those responsible for both family and child (20 percent), and those responsible for family, child, and child-caring person (22 percent). Those responsible for work with the natural family constituted only 10 percent of the sample. The remaining 8 percent were supervisors, either carrying cases or reporting on behalf of workers who had left. Over time, the most noteworthy change is reflected in the fact that those who specialized in work with the natural families declined from 14 percent at Time 1 to only 3 percent at the fourth cycle.

Work pressure
Since the conditions under which these workers carried out their responsibilities were expected to have a direct effect on the service given the children and their families, respondents were questioned in detail about

the pressures they felt. Of them, 17 percent were carrying relatively low case loads of 15 or fewer children; 53 percent reported case loads ranging from 16 to 30, with the median for the entire sample between 21 and 25; 30 percent reported case loads over 30. Again, the Time 1 workers differed from all the others in that their case loads were higher. The median for them was 36, while at the succeeding cycle the median dropped to 25 and remained there.

As additional indicators of case pressure, workers were asked how much time they spent on each of eight major tasks common to most child welfare workers: field travel, recording, visiting or observing children, visiting or interviewing parents, discussions with foster parents or counselors, participation in supervisory conferences and staff meetings, and contacts with other agencies. For many, even approximate time estimates were difficult, but most could respond with subjective judgments as to whether the time spent at each task was "too much," "too little," or "about right." Of those who could give time estimates, only 52 percent indicated that the better part of their time was devoted to direct contact with clients while 42 percent indicated that the better part of their time was devoted to matters classed as "administrative" (writing reports, recording, traveling, etc.). Workers were most satisfied with the amount of time given to supervisory conferences (83 percent), to conferences with child-caring persons (80 percent), and to travel (80 percent). The extent of satisfaction was lower for the amount of time spent with outside agencies (76 percent) and in staff meetings (74 percent).

Dissatisfaction was more marked in relation to direct contact with the child; only 56 percent of the workers thought the amount of time they spent with the children was adequate. The same was true for contact with natural families. The largest number of complaints were made about time spent on recording, where only 52 percent of the workers reported satisfaction with the time allocated to this task. Of those complaining, two-thirds thought they spent too much time in this area while a third thought they spent too little.

Over time, dissatisfaction with the number of hours spent in contact with the family and in travel increased. Complaints about the number of staff meetings and contacts with other agencies decreased, while complaints about the number of hours spent with children, with child-caring persons, with supervisors, and on recording tended to remain at the same level.

Asked to assess the degree of pressure they felt, 56 percent of the workers sampled said they found their work loads manageable, while 28 percent felt they were under moderate pressure and 16 percent felt they were under heavy pressure. Of those who acknowledged pressure, the largest group (23 percent) attributed it, not surprisingly, to high case loads, but almost as many respondents (22 percent) described their pressures as internal—generated by their own standards of service. Despite shifts from the public to the voluntary agencies and lower case loads, the picture of the sample with respect to pressure and its sources did not vary markedly over the successive time cycles.

Pressure was not necessarily related to the degree of satisfaction; 62 percent of the respondents claimed to derive considerable satisfaction from their work, 32 percent said they derived some satisfaction, while only 6 percent said they derived none. Again, the response did not vary substantially over time despite the changes in the nature of the agency sample and the concomitant changes in working conditions.

Of the total sample, 36 percent of the respondents described their satisfactions as rooted in working directly with children while 16 percent derived satisfaction from work with natural families. These proportions, however, differed considerably with each cycle. At Time 1, the proportion of workers who related their satisfactions to working with children was the same (28 percent) as those whose satisfactions were focused on the natural family. At Time 2, the proportion deriving their satisfactions from working with children rose to 41 percent and reached 49 percent at the final cycle. By contrast, the proportion basing their satisfactions on work with the family dropped to 16 percent at Time 2 and continued to decline until it constituted only 3 percent at the final cycle.

Knowledge of clients
Given the workers' limited experience, the pressures to which they were subjected, and the emergency nature of many of the placements, how well did these workers know these children and their families, especially at the time of the initial decision to place?

At each cycle of data collection, the interviewing and senior coding staff made a series of judgments about the workers' knowledge of each case. Criteria for assessing the workers' knowledge included the extent to which they were able to supply the data required by the interview and the ease with which they did so—for example, when detailed information would be given spontaneously, without resorting to a review of the record or to questioning the supervisor.

At Time 1, the workers as a group differed markedly in their knowledge of the child's history before his placement and their knowledge of his current state. Only 31 percent were able to give with certainty a detailed account of his past history, including dates of major changes, while 24 percent were judged to have general knowledge but could not supply such details as times of major changes, and 39 percent had some knowledge of the child's history but expressed uncertainty in the form of such comments as "He was always in the care of his mother, as far as I know." With 6 percent of the children, only the current situation was known to the worker.

On the other hand, most workers (77 percent) whose functions required direct contact with the child were able to give a detailed description of the child's current condition. A little over a fourth of this group were considered exceptionally knowledgeable—i.e., able to give details well beyond the requirements of the interview schedule.

As would be expected with children more settled in placement, nearly all workers in the later cycles were able to give adequate accounts of the child's current state. The proportion of those able to go beyond the requirements of the interview rose at each cycle, reaching 42 percent at Time 4.

Cross-tabulation of the knowledge level of the worker for each cycle showed a significant difference between Time 1 and Time 2, in that the number of cases in which worker knowledge improved was 12 percent higher than those in which it declined. The difference rose to 15 percent at Time 3 and 21 percent at Time 4.

Summary

The 1,074 workers who supplied the data for this study were widely scattered among public and voluntary (largely sectarian) agencies. Involvement of the public sector declined over time. The largest number were involved in providing long-term foster home care, followed by those in long-term institutional care, while the smallest number were involved in agencies giving temporary care.

Workers were typically under 30, white, female, and single. Slightly less than half the sample had no training beyond a bachelor's degree, while one-third had partial training and approximately one-fifth had a master's degree. The typical level of experience was two years. The level of training and experience increased over time.

Most workers were relatively unspecialized in their assignments; they worked with natural parents, with children and foster parents, or with institutional counselors. Over time, the proportion of workers assigned to work with natural families decreased.

Case loads for Time 1 workers were relatively high, but dropped in later cycles. Nearly half the workers reported working under conditions of at least moderate or high pressure while a third reported that the satisfaction derived was limited. In relation to specific tasks, workers complained most of excessive time spent in recording and too little spent in direct contact with children and with natural families. Despite changes in agency auspices and improvement in such objective measures of pressure as the size of the case load, the extent to which subjective pressure and dissatisfaction was reported remained relatively constant over time.

The largest proportion of workers reported that their satisfactions were based on direct contact with children; those finding satisfaction in work with natural families declines over time. Their knowledge of the child's background was relatively weak in the first stage of the study, but in other areas, and in later time cycles, workers' knowledge of their clients—both child and family—appeared to be more than adequate.

chapter three

FAMILIES IN THE EYES OF
THEIR WORKERS

ALTHOUGH IT IS THE CHILDREN who are placed, their families are de-scribed first, since it is their problems which create the situation requiring placement and it is they, more than their children, who present the problems their social workers must deal with.

In the Time 1 sample, agency data covered 458 families.[1] As was ex-pected, the size of the sample declined with time as children were dis-charged home or placed in adoption. Family data covered 397 families at Time 2, 378 at Time 3, and 263 at Time 4. The amount of data avail-able on these families varied, depending on the worker's knowledge; data were minimal when based entirely on limited contacts with workers or on case records, and maximal when workers had extensive direct contact. In most instances, it was the mother with whom the worker had contact. Less frequently they worked with both parents, the father alone, or various combinations of parents and other relatives.

Demographic Variables

In relating client data to agency data, four demographic variables were used to determine the extent to which the outcomes the study was con-cerned with were related to client characteristics, as well as to agency-based phenomena. These variables were the mother's age, race, socioeco-

1. The family sample at Time 1 is described in detail in Shirley Jenkins and Elaine Nor-man, *Filial Deprivation and Foster Care* (New York: Columbia University Press, 1972), ch. 2.

nomic status, and marital status, based on data collected by the family phase of the study. All other variables describing the family were derived from the data provided by the workers.

The mothers involved in the study were relatively young. At Time 1, half were between the ages of 25 and 35. Over time, the size of the youngest group (those under 25 at placement) declined from 19 to 14 percent while the oldest (those over 36 at placement) increased from 30 to 38 percent; this suggests that the younger mothers were more likely to place children for adoption or take their children home.

At Time 1, 40 percent of the mothers in the sample were black, 27 percent Puerto Rican, and 33 percent white.[2] Despite the attrition of the sample, these proportions remained quite stable, varying by no more than two percentage points for each of the subsequent cycles.

At Time 1, the socioeconomic status of 24 percent of the mothers was described as "low," [3] and 45 percent as "high"; the remaining 31 percent was placed in the "middle" group. Not surprisingly, the porportion of mothers with a low socioeconomic status increased somewhat to 27 percent at the final cycle while those of high socioeconomic status, with the greater potential for discharge, declined to 37 percent.

At Time 1, 37 percent of the mothers were single (never married) while 35 percent were separated from their husbands. 18 percent were currently married while the remaining 10 percent were divorced or widowed. Over time, the proportion of single mothers was relatively stable while the proportion in the "separated" category increased to 43 percent. Again, because they had a greater potential for taking their children home, the proportion of married mothers declined to 12 percent, and the divorced or widowed to 7 percent.[4]

Reason for Placement

With one exception, all reasons for placement given by the worker, centered on problems presented by one or both parents or parent substitutes,

2. The "white" group includes five mothers described as "Asiatic" or "others."
3. The criteria on which these categories were based are described in Jenkins and Norman, *Filial Deprivation*, pp. 43–51. It should be understood that almost the entire sample consisted of families whose socioeconomic status is low relative to the population in general. The designations of "low," "middle," and "high" refer to their status within the sample.
4. The reader should understand that differences in the frequency distributions given in the various reports from other phases of the Child Welfare Research Program are the result of differences in sample loss.

most frequently the natural mother. The exception—personality problems or disturbing behavior in the child himself—accounted for 11 percent of the cases. As Table 3.1 indicates, these problems varied considerably with no single problem predominant.

At Time 2, workers were asked whether the child was continuing in care for the same reason he was originally placed. For 69 percent of the

TABLE 3.1

Reason for Placement as Given by Agency Workers [a]

Reason	Percent (N = 458)
Unwillingness or inability to continue care [b]	25
Neglect or abuse	19
Mental illness	13
Unwillingness or inability to assume care [c]	13
Child's behavior/personality problems	11
Physical illness	9
Arrest or imprisonment	4
Family conflict [d]	3
Drug Addiction [e]	2
Alcoholism	1
	100

[a] Percentages are based on the family sample since siblings were almost invariably placed for the same reason.
[b] This category consists of cases of abandonment, both temporary and continued, and cases in which the mother asked for placement, claiming inability to continue care. In all instances, mothers had been caring for the children before placement.
[c] This category consists largely of unmarried mothers who asked for placement during pregnancy or shortly after delivery and did not care for the child themselves.
[d] This category included a variety of situations, most commonly those in which grandparents refused to permit an unmarried mother to take a child home or in which a lover or stepfather refused to have children of a previous marriage in the home.
[e] This category includes only cases in which the parent's addiction was given as the reason for placement. Since "reason for placement" was defined as the immediate precipitating event, other categories, such as "arrest" and "imprisonment," also include drug addicts.

children, the precipitating reason was reported to be unmodified, but the proportion varied by reason for placement. "Unwillingness to assume care" was the reason least likely to be changed by Time 2. The reasons most likely to have been modified were physical or mental illness of the mother; in these cases mothers had been discharged from the hospital but doubts remained about their capacity to care for their children. There were also instances where housing or income problems prevented them from taking the children home.

At Times 3 and 4, workers were asked why the child was continuing in care. As Table 3.2 indicates, the result was a somewhat different series of reasons.

An analysis of changes over time showed many differences in the reasons given when data from each time cycle are compared. This is to be expected when one considers that different respondents are involved in the majority of cases, most of which involve complex problems that can legitimately be defined in a variety of ways. Even so, it is worth noting that two categories of reasons for placement show a greater degree of sta-

TABLE 3.2

Reasons for Continuation in Placement

Reason	Percent at Time 3 (N = 378)	Percent at Time 4 (N = 263)
Mother or father are unable to meet child's needs, care for child, supervise, make plans	28	38
Mother or father are unstable	15	13
Total abandonment; no contact between child and family	14	13
Mother or father have mental illness	12	8
Mother or father rejects child	11	3
Child is emotionally disturbed	9	4
Plans for adoption are in process	8	19
Other	3	2
	100	100

bility than the others. Of the 41 children placed for emotional distur- bance and still in care at Time 3, 26 continued in care for the same reason. The same was true for 54 children placed because their mother was mentally ill: half were seen as continuing in care for the same reason. This relative stability continues to hold at Time 4 for the children of the mentally ill but not for the behavior disturbances. Of the 18 emotionally disturbed children in care at the final cycle, all but four were seen as con- tinuing for reasons having to do with parental incapacity, not with the nature of the original problem.

Legal status

Another important aspect of placement is the legal status of the parents, since their retention of rights over their children effectively controls the agency's basic decisions about discharge, continued long-term care, and adoption. At Time 1, 79 percent of the placements were based on the voluntary authorization of the parents. For 21 percent, placement had been ordered by a judge of the Family Court with continuation or termination subject to court decision.

In general, this picture did not change much over time; at each cycle, about one-quarter of the children were in placements that involved the Court. At each point in time, six or seven percent of the children were discharged from court jurisdiction to their parents or to the Commissioner of Welfare, but by Time 4 a similar proportion had become involved with the Court for the first time. These were often cases in which agencies took legal action to terminate parental rights and make adoption possible. In other instances children who had been at home were taken to Court as "Persons in Need of Supervision," because of truancy or other behavior difficulties. Thus the Court was involved in the problems of placement to much the same extent over the five-year time span covered by the study, but the nature of the involvement varied over time.

Siblings

Seventy-five percent of the study subjects had siblings; 33 percent of the 345 families who had more than one child placed the study subject but none of his siblings, in 23 percent of the cases some siblings were placed while others remained at home, and in 43 percent, all the children in the family were placed.

Virtually all situations that precipitated placement affected at least some of the siblings as much as the study subjects, with the exception of those for which the reason was the child's behavior. Of the 45 children initially placed for this reason, only 7 had other siblings in placement.

Of the 221 families in which more than one sibling was placed, 41 percent had all children placed with the same agency. The rest were either entirely separated from their siblings or were separated from some but not others.

The large majority (81 percent) of the study subjects with siblings held the same status with respect to placement at Time 1 as the sibling—the siblings were continued in care, transferred to other agencies, or sent home at the same time. The remaining 19 percent were either sent home or transferred at different dates—or else one child remained in care while the others were discharged. The most common reason for differential treatment was the fact that one child had special problems, usually of an emotional nature, which made it desirable for him either to go home earlier or to remain in care longer than his siblings. Next in frequency were those situations in which the mother was unable to take all the children home at the same time, either for reasons of health or inadequate housing. Siblings were transferred to long-term care at different dates, usually because no single placement was available for a large family unit.

Over time, the proportion of children with the same status as their siblings declined and the proportion of those with a different status rose. Again, the most common reason for this differentiation was the inability of the mother to take all the children home at once.

Accessibility of the family to the agency

At Time 1, mothers were known to the agency in 94 percent of the cases and fathers in 60 percent. Agency contact extended further than the parents for only a third of the families. For 4 percent of the children, parents were never reached and contact was limited to other relatives or friends. For 2 percent, it was not possible to reach any family member.

There were varying reasons for lack of contact with parents or for contact only with other relatives or friends. Most frequently, the severity of the mother's disorder (chronic schizophrenia, long-standing drug addiction, or alcoholism) required that she be institutionalized, making direct communication impossible. In a few instances, the children placed were foundlings or had been surrendered immediately after birth, while in others the mother was deceased and the father had long since deserted.

Workers appeared to regard relatives as dubious resources and had little motivation to work with them. The most common reason for relatives' lack of involvement seemed to be that they had already "done their part" by taking one sibling into their homes, and did not wish to become involved with the others—at least not to the point of being parent-substitutes. Despite the presence on many records of names and addresses of several relatives or friends, relatives were apparently contacted infrequently and were worked with only if there was a possibility they would assume responsibility.

For all three measurement cycles which followed the first year of placement, agency contact continued to be limited to the mother in the largest proportion of cases—about one-third at each cycle. An analysis of the changes in the extent of family contact indicates that, at Time 2, 51 percent of the families had maintained the pattern seen at Time 1. For 20 percent, agency contact included more family members than at Time 1, but for a larger proportion (29 percent) fewer members were being seen. At Time 4, workers were seeing fewer members of the family than they had been seeing at Time 1 in 37 percent of the cases, and more members in 28 percent.

Data on the degree of contact after intake with the mother show a similar picture. At Time 1, 38 percent of the mothers had had relatively frequent contact with their workers (five or more interviews over the time period covered), and 37 percent had less intensive contact (one to four interviews). For 3 percent, contact was limited to telephone calls or brief encounters while visiting the child, leaving 22 percent with whom there was no contact at all.

The proportion of mothers having no contact with the agency rose slightly at each of the subsequent time cycles, reaching 26 percent at Time 4. The percentage of new "dropouts"—mothers with whom there was contact at the time of the earlier measure and none at the later measure—also rose with each cycle, from 11 percent at Time 2 to 16 percent at Time 4. For those who were in contact, there was a decline in frequency: 45 percent of the families active at Time 2 had less contact with the agency than they had had at Time 1 and 20 percent had more frequent contact. The picture was reversed between Time 2 and Time 3, when 36 percent of the families had increased contact with the agency and 24 percent had less. By Time 4, however, the picture was similar to what it had been at Time 2—there was more deterioration than improvement: 41 percent of the mothers seen at Time 3 had less contact with the agency by Time 4, and 23 percent had more.

As indicated earlier, contact with the fathers after intake was even less frequent than with the mothers. In the first year of placement, no contact with the father was possible for 38 percent of the families, either because his whereabouts were unknown or because he had left the city or was institutionalized. This occurred most commonly in the case of unmarried mothers planning to place their children in foster care or for adoption— no father in this group was seen for more than one or two interviews, if he was seen at all. For 15 percent of the families, the father's whereabouts were known, but either no effort was made to reach him or such efforts were not successful. For 9 percent, contacts were limited to telephone calls, brief visits, or conversations while accompanying the mother on a visit. Contact with the father in the form of at least one full interview or more occurred in only 37 percent of the families.

Frequent contact (five or more interviews) with the father was most common where the reason for placement was the mother's mental illness, drug addiction, or alcoholism. When the children were placed for behavior problems, fathers were seen in the large majority of cases (71 percent). The fathers were seen in such cases more than in any others, and those seen were equally divided among those who were contacted on a very limited basis, those seen for only one or two interviews, and those seen for three interviews or more. It would seem that the father's involvement with the child welfare agency was likely to be extensive only if he carried the major responsibility for the children.

Over time, an increasing proportion of fathers dropped out of the picture. At Time 2, 33 percent of the fathers had been continuously absent. For the children still in placement at Time 3, 44 percent of the fathers had been continuously out of touch since the earlier measure. Unlike the mothers, there was at no point an increase in frequency of contact for those who were in touch with the agency.

Contact Between Family and Child [5]

Maintaining the relationship between family and child through regular contact is considered a vital factor in the child's adjustment to placement. In this respect, workers at Time 1 reported that 5 percent of the children had no contact at all with their families after placement, usually because adoption was being planned. For 8 percent, contacts were controlled or restricted by the agency for a variety of reasons, of which the most common was drunkenness or other disturbing behavior on the part of the parent. The large majority of children, however, had at least minimal contact during the first year.

The proportion of children having no contact with their families at all rose sharply to 25 percent at Time 2 and continued to rise slightly at each succeeding cycle, reaching 29 percent at the final one. On the other

5. The reader should not confuse worker contact with families (reported in the preceding section) with contact between families and children. Workers went to the homes of parents and relatives who may not have visited their children at all. On the other hand, in some settings—particularly institutional ones—it was possible for parents to visit children at times when they could avoid contact with workers.

hand, the children whose contacts were limited to parents declined to 21 percent by Time 4. The proportion of children having contact with members of their families other than the parents rose over time as they grew older and more mobile. At Time 4, 50 percent of the children had contact with members of their families other than their parents, including siblings not in placement.

Although many children in placement maintain some degree of contact with various members of their families, it is nevertheless the mother's visiting behavior that is most significant. Here the picture is less encouraging. During the period covered by Time 1, the largest group of mothers (41 percent) visited at all or nearly all the opportunities provided by the agency; the visits of 12 percent were described as frequent but irregular, while the visits of 17 percent were described as occasional or rare. In 13 percent of the cases the mother did not visit at all, although she was apparently able to do so; 10 percent of the mothers were either ill, institutionalized, or in some restricting situation which did not permit them to visit. The remaining cases were those in which the mother was deceased or where the information is missing.

Of the mothers who were able to visit but did not do so, about a third had surrendered, or were seriously considering surrendering, their children for adoption, and were therefore not encouraged to visit. An almost equally large number of mothers had abandoned their children some time before placement and had never returned. (In some instances, their whereabouts were known either to the father or the agency. They were frequently known to have started new families.) In any case, their failure to visit was apparently part of an established pattern of rejection, in contrast to other mothers whose desertion was episodic and who reestablished contact after placement. Another group of nonvisiting mothers were drug-addict prostitutes whose reasons for failing to visit were usually not explicitly given. The workers, however, thought it probable that they were avoiding all organizations or official bodies to reduce the danger of arrest. Yet another group consisted of retarded or mentally ill mothers, whose limitations did not permit them to travel.

At Time 2, the proportion of mothers who visited at every opportunity dropped to 33 percent and continued to decline in the later cycles—to 23 percent at the final one. At each point, the proportion of mothers whose visiting pattern became worse was considerably greater than those whose visiting pattern improved. Between Time 1 and Time 2, 47 percent of the mothers were visiting less, while 24 percent were visiting more. At Time 3, 44 percent were visiting less while 18 percent were visiting more. At Time 4, 26 percent were visiting less while 14 percent were visiting more.

Of the fathers known to the agency, 48 percent visited at every opportunity at Time 1, 8 percent visited frequently but irregularly, while 17 percent came only rarely or occasionally; 22 percent did not visit at all, although, as far as could be determined from the available information, they were in a position to do so. In 4 percent of the cases, the father was ill or institutionalized and unable to visit. Thus, the father's pattern was initially slightly more extreme than the mothers; they were likely to visit either as often as permitted or not at all.

Over time, however, the actively involved fathers, although they were small in number, maintained a stable pattern of maximum visiting. By Time 4, maximum visiting characterized two-thirds of the small group of fathers who continued to be involved with their children in placement.

Family Reactions to Placement

In general, Time 1 workers reported that the majority of parents accepted placement as the solution to their immediate problem. Of 182 families where children were already in long-term placement at Time 1, 57 percent of the parents were said to accept it completely. For 21 percent, there was evidence of mixed feelings—some resentment or anxiety but not open opposition. For 6 percent, there were differing opinions within the family; usually one parent accepted placement, the other opposed it. For 16 percent, the attitude was basically negative. They neither wanted nor accepted placement, but as a rule had no choice in the matter, because the situation was in the hands of the court.

Members of those families who objected to placement did so for various reasons: because the child's placement, especially when he entered long-term care, underscored a family's own physical or mental problems, serving as an indication that early recovery was not expected; because a father or another close relative was unable to see the mother's limitations in caring for the children; because the decision for placement had been made while they were institutionalized and lacked control. But the most common incidents discernible from the workers' reports were the denials of parents charged with abuse or neglect. Even when they did acknowledge the severity of the disciplinary method they used on their children, they could not understand why placement was needed. The following cases serve as illustrations:

CASE 1:   A ten-year-old girl placed together with her sister when the Bureau of Attendance of the city's public school system filed a petition of neglect: her mother denied most of the allegations, and rationalized her daughters' truancy on grounds that she was needed to care for infant cousins. The mother also denied that she had participated in a drinking party, as cited in the petition, but also said she would not allow it to recur. The psychiatrist noted in his summary: "This family wants to stick together, conceals or denies (perhaps even to themselves) any difficulties, and presented a united front in their interview. They see the Court as a threat, rather than a help."

CASE 2:   A four-year-old girl placed when siblings died in a fire: family had been under supervision of the Court as a "neglect" case; the mother was considered dull and functioning on a retarded level. She displayed no emotion when reacting to the Court's decision; she just repeated that she could care for the children and therefore did not want them placed. Physical abuse was justified because "the children were bad and she had to beat them." She denied that she had left them alone.

When one considers the family as a whole, including those in temporary as well as those in long-term placement, 39 percent had some degree of discomfort with the agency goals, even if most were not in total opposition to them.

Over time, 40 to 50 percent of the families were consisistent in their attitudes; the number of those whose attitudes become more positive than they had been initially was about equal to the number of those who became more negative. At each cycle, about one-third of the families receiving service were described as having mixed feelings about continuing to have children in care. Those whose attitudes were more clearly negative varied from 7 to 14 percent.

Family's Role in the Placement Problems

As in any system of services, some families present problems more difficult to deal with than do others. For analytic purposes, the extent to which a family was problematic for the agency was based on the presence or absence of consensus among the persons involved in the placement process. In other words, for a case in which the family wanted placement, workers agreed that it was the best available solution to the problems presented, and the child seemed to be getting along well in care, consensus existed, and the case was considered "nonproblematic." Situations in which some or all members of the family were unwilling to leave the child in placement, the workers involved were not certain that placement was the optimal form of treatment, or the child himself was resistant to remaining in care were described as "nonconsensus" or "problematic."

In many instances there was more than one major problem, the source of which could either be within the family, the agency, or the child. As will be seen later, the largest group of cases were those in which a combination of family and agency factors produced the strain in question. Of all the cases considered "problematic" at Time 1, family problems, major or secondary, were seen in 48 percent. The proportion remained at the same level until Time 4, when nearly two-thirds of the problems of children still in care were attributed to the family.

As Table 3.3 indicates, the worker's doubt about the mother's capacity

TABLE 3.3

Major Problems in "Problematic" Families

	Time 1 (N = 219)		Time 2 (N = 165)		Time 3 (N = 161)		Time 4 (N = 133)	
	Rank	%	Rank	%	Rank	%	Rank	%
Uncertainty about mother's capacity to care for child	1	32	2	19	1	23	1.5	21
Mother is indecisive, resistant, or passive about taking child home	2	20	—	—	—	—	—	—
Uncertainty about other family members' ability to care	3.5	19	—	—	—	—	—	—
Resistance of parents to placement	3.5	19	1	29	—	—	—	—
Lack of contact with parents; difficult to plan	—	—	3	18	2	21	1.5	21
Mother's indifference; rejection	—	—	—	—	3	16	—	—
Incomplete recovery from mental illness	—	—	—	—	—	—	3	14
"Problems" in other categories		10		34		40		34

to care for child was either the first or second most common family-based problem at each point. The lack of sufficient contact with parents to enable the worker to make plans emerged as the third problem in order of frequency at Time 2, and increased in importance until by the final cycle it was equal in dimensions to the first-named problem. Parental resistance to placement as such or to particular types of placement (as in the case of parents who accepted institutional care, but not foster homes) was the third most common problem in order of frequency at Time 1, ranked first at Time 2, and then ceased to be significant—apparently because most such parents had succeeded in removing their children from care by the third year after the initial placement or else had become resigned to placement.

Workers' Perceptions of Mothers

Up to this point, most of the data reported have been based on fairly objective, observable facts such as frequency of contacts between worker and mother and between mother and child. The workers' more qualitative and subjective judgments about these women's capacity for motherhood and their attitudes toward a plan for their children obviously played a major role in the workers' decision whether to plan toward returning the child home or toward long-term placement or for adoption.

Maternal adequacy

Of 326 mothers with whom workers had sufficient contact at Time 1 to make a judgment, only 22 percent impressed their workers as adequate. For 33 percent, the workers had mixed feelings, and described both positive and negative aspects of mothering such as the ability to give good physical care, offset by inability to respond emotionally. For the largest group (37 percent), mothers were considered by their workers to be very inadequate as mothers, able at best to give only minimal care. The remaining 8 percent were mothers who had not functioned in that capacity at all, having placed their first child at birth. This latter group was about evenly divided between those whose potential as mothers was considered good by the worker and those about whom they had doubts. Not surprisingly, the mothers most likely to be considered adequate were those who had placed their children because of physical illness and those least likely to be considered adequate were those charged with neglect.

In later phases of the study, the proportion of mothers seen as inadequate rose to 52 percent by the final cycle with a corresponding decrease in those seen as adequate, since the latter were obviously the mothers who were likely to have taken their children home. For the small groups where comparisons could be made at succeeding times, the indications were that the largest proportion of these judgments (41–45 percent) tended to remain the same, with a slight tendency for the proportion whose assessment improved to be greater than those whose assessment deteriorated.

Attitudes toward the agency

When Time 1 workers were asked how they thought the mother viewed the agency, a little over half expressed the opinion that mothers saw the agency primarily in positive terms as a source of help. About a quarter were described as viewing the agency as a convenience, a resource for temporary care. Twenty-one percent were perceived by the workers as viewing the agency in negative terms, as usurpers of their rights to care for their children.

Over time, about half the mothers were seen as unchanged in their attitude, but for those who did change, the number who became more negative was higher than those who became more positive. At Time 3, for example, 30 percent of the mothers known to the worker were described as holding more negative views of the agency than they had earlier in contrast to 19 percent who were now perceived as seeing the agency in positive terms.

Outlook for cooperation

When asked how they assessed the prospect of working with the mothers they knew, workers at Time 1 thought the outlook was good for 48 percent, but their optimism was guarded for about a quarter of this group. In these cases, workers thought that mothers could be helped only if casework were intensive or involved a skilled worker or a psychiatrist or, at the very least, constituted part of a sustained effort on the part of some agency. In some instances, workers thought the outlook favorable only if the worker could accept and work within the mother's limitations or if there were some basic changes in the family situation. One worker said, for example, of one young mother with an out-of-wedlock infant that she might be helped to make a decision about her child's future "if she can escape the grandmother."

For another 18 percent of the mothers, workers' feelings were even more mixed; they discerned motivation on the mother's part for continued contact but were not optimistic about its ultimate effects. For nearly a fourth of the mothers, workers thought the outlook was poor, since the mothers either resisted contact, did not appear interested, or else were barred by problems from effective contact.

At Time 2, the proportion of mothers about whom workers were pessimistic increased somewhat, then rose to nearly a third at Time 3, and dropped again to 21 percent at the final cycle, when the number of involved mothers was comparatively small. The relative strength of tendencies toward optimism or pessimism fluctuated at each time cycle, suggesting that the workers' impressions varied considerably over time.

When asked to predict whether the child's mother was likely to be a "dropout" (one who loses contact with the agency once the child is placed) workers at Time 1 were relatively optimistic. In 54 percent of the cases discussed, they thought it unlikely or impossible. They saw some likelihood that the mother would lose contact for 18 percent of the cases, and for another 18 percent thought that the mothers had already "dropped out."

At Time 2, worker optimism apparently increased, since two-thirds of the mothers involved were expected to remain in touch; but this expectation diminished in the later phases of the study. By Time 4, workers were confident that mothers would remain in contact for 47 percent of the active cases. Comparisons between predictions made at successive points in time for the same mothers indicated that predictions become more consistent over time. Workers at Time 2 made the same prediction as Time 1 workers for 39 percent of the cases but Time 4 workers made the same prediction as Time 3 workers for 50 percent.

Changes in workers' assessments were obviously significant, since they affected the child's chances for discharge. A review of 50 cases in which workers' assessments changed from positive to more neutral or negative, either between Time 1 and Time 2 or between Time 2 and Time 3, suggests a number of trends. The predominant ones were those in which workers appear to have overestimated the client's capacity for motherhood, her willingness to take the child home, or her willingness to be helped. In some cases, new evidence appeared that the emotional disturbance of the mother was more severe than it originally seemed to be.

In some cases, workers initially seemed much taken with the intelligence, education, talents, or charm of some of the younger mothers, and minimized more disturbing evidence—such as histories of drug addiction and mental illness. Later they were disillusioned when the mother failed to take the child home as planned or did so and brought him back to be placed again. In the later stages of placement, some cases involved mothers who, after a long history of severe disturbances, seemed to be doing well in new jobs or training programs. The workers responded to the new situation by anticipating discharge in the near future. By the time the workers were interviewed for the study, the mothers had lost their jobs or had been dropped by the training programs, and the worker's optimism had diminished. The following cases are illustrative:

CASE 1:   *Time 2:* An eight-year-old girl was placed in a foster home when her mother deserted. The mother later reappeared, and at Time 2 the worker was "very positive about mother." The mother had come to the agency immediately when the worker wrote to her, and said she wanted to see the child; she indicated that she wanted her home. She was working, and had two children living with her, with whom she had a good relationship. She seemed responsible, made a good impression, showed no sign of emotional disturbance. The worker thought the child would go home at the end of the school year (six months from the date of the interview) if the mother maintained her interest.

Time 3: Two years later, the child was still in care and was expected to remain. The same worker reported that the plan for discharge was dropped, when the mother began having difficulty handling the child on visits home. Eventually she lost contact with the agency altogether. The worker now described her as "very dull, dependent, and immature," "never able to hold or initiate a conversation."

CASE 2:   *Time 2:* A three-year-old boy was placed in a foster home after the mother was charged with neglect. At Time 2, the worker assigned had seen the mother twice, exchanged letters with her, described her as very intelligent and aware of child's needs. Feeling the child should be with her, the worker supported the mother in her wish to have the child. The mother had obtained a job with a public agency. The worker was disturbed, however, by the mother's insistence that there was no need for the child to be placed; the description of neglect had been very detailed. A court psychiatrist felt that the mother— bright and imaginative—could function at a better level with help. The worker said the mother had a very warm attitude toward her: "She thinks I'm great."

Time 3: At Time 3, the child had been discharged. The same worker described the mother as functioning very well as a mother. She was still working but had married a handicapped man, had two more children, had full financial responsibility for the family, but did not seem to mind it. Her attitude toward the worker was now described as "superficially positive." At the end of this period, the child reentered care and the worker was interviewed to update the situation. She reported that the half-siblings were also placed—again on charges of neglect; they were left alone all day and the child was not sent to school. The mother was still working, but the worker did not know whether she were still living with her husband. The mother said she wanted to visit the children, but did not. There was some suspicion that she was taking drugs. Toward the agency, she put on "A front of pleasantness," was not cooperative. The worker now predicted the child would remain in care for the rest of his childhood.

Workers' Perceptions of Fathers

Whenever appropriate, the questions related to the mother were also asked about the father. Because the sample of involved fathers was initially much smaller than that of mothers, and also declined over time, the trends were less clear.

Fathers' adequacy

At Time 1, the family sample included 142 fathers with whom the workers had sufficient contact. Half of these fathers were considered inadequate; the workers thought they had some interest in their children but not enough to meet the youngster's needs. The other half were considered adequate—i.e., concerned and responsible.

The number of adequate fathers was much higher than that of mothers, presumably because the mothers' problems affected the placement directly and were more visible than the fathers'. The relative mobility of men in urban society also permits the totally inadequate father to desert the family. Thus, the selective factors operating in placement result in the fact that the fathers who do maintain contact with the agency are more likely to be responsible, concerned parents, who are forced to place their children for lack of adequate mothers or mother substitutes. Over time, as the sample size diminishes, trends reflecting the continuing adequacy of fathers are difficult to discern.

Fathers' attitudes toward agency

At Time 1, fathers were more inclined than mothers to see the agency in a helping role. Of the small group of fathers who continued to be known

to the workers, the majority were at each subsequent time cycle reported
to hold consistently positive views toward the agencies caring for their
children.

Outlook for working with father

At Time 1, workers were optimistic about working with 48 percent of the
fathers, had mixed feelings about 22 percent and were pessimistic about
30 percent. As with attitudes toward the agency, the proportion of active
fathers about whom the workers were optimistic increased. Thus, although actual contact, as reported earlier, may diminish, the worker's attitude does not necessarily become more negative as it does in the case of
the mothers.

Summary

The "families" with whom placement workers dealt were generally
headed by relatively young mothers, either single or separated from their
husbands, of nonwhite origins, and low socioeconomic status. They
usually placed their children in foster care at a time of crisis or severe
emotional strain. Whatever the nature of the events precipitating placement, the most common reason for its continuation was the worker's
opinion that these mothers were unable to assume their full responsibility.

These placements were at least formally of a voluntary nature, but a
significant minority were made under the jurisdiction of the court. Placement frequently involved an entire family unit in addition to the children
selected for the study. The siblings initially occupied the same status with
regard to placement as the study children. The tendency for the workers
to limit their contacts to parents only—particularly the mother—became
more marked over time. Frequency of contact with mothers declined, as
did contact with fathers.

Family reactions to placement were usually seen as accepting, but a
substantial minority were perceived to have mixed or negative feelings—a
pattern that remained fairly consistent over time. The key problem for the
particularly difficult families was that of uncertainty about the mothers'
capacity to care for their children, and it remained the key problem over
time.

The majority of mothers were seen as of doubtful adequacy, a proportion that increased over time. Initially, half the mothers were perceived as viewing the agency in positive terms, as a source of help; but over time, attitudes were seen to become more negative. Similarly, the workers' optimism that mothers would remain in contact with the agency tended to diminish. Not all responses to questions of this nature showed consistent deterioration, but there was certainly no clear positive trend.

The workers' relationships with the few active fathers were somewhat different. Here, evaluations of the father and of the attitudes he was perceived to hold were somewhat more positive and consistent over time. However, they affected only a small proportion of the children involved.

In general, then, the picture of worker–family relations within the agency network was basically one of deterioration over time, both with respect to frequency of contact and to the evaluations of parents. Here the key problem for the worker was dealing with the ambiguity of definitions of adequate parenthood.

chapter four

CHILDREN IN THE EYES OF THEIR WORKERS

W E HAVE EXAMINED some of the characteristics of the families whose breakdowns precipitated their children into foster care, but what of the children themselves? Clearly, most children placed have lived with poverty or near-poverty all their lives, and by definition have suffered at least one major crisis in their lives and often more than one. How much damage do the workers see in these children and how do their perceptions change over time?

Demographic Characteristics

The child sample [1] was originally evenly divided between boys and girls. Over time, girls left care slightly more frequently than boys, so that the Time 4 sample was 55 percent boys and 45 percent girls.

Twenty percent of the study children entered care at birth or before their first birthday, 33 percent were preschool children, 37 percent were of elementary school age (6–11). The remaining 10 percent were between ages 12 and 14. There was no significant difference in this age distribution at Time 2, but by Times 3 and 4 the children in the highest age categories were discharged, having reached the limits of agency responsibility. For the final sample, 25 percent were children who had been infants at placement. The proportion of children who were preschoolers

1. The child sample is described in greater detail in David Fanshel and Eugene B. Shinn, *Children in Foster Care* (New York: Columbia University Press, Forthcoming).

when placed rose 2 percent, while the proportion of those who were already in school dropped 2 percent. The size of the oldest group declined
to 5 percent.

Data on the socioeconomic origins of the children obviously reflected
those given on the parents in chapter 3 and showed the same changes
over time, in which the proportion of children of relatively high socioeconomic status declined by the final cycle.

The original sample was evenly divided between children born in and
out of wedlock. There was little change in this respect in the first two
years of placement, but in both the later cycles the in-wedlock children
were more likely to be discharged, leaving the proportions in the final
sample as 60 percent out of wedlock and 40 percent in wedlock.

In terms of ethnicity, the largest group of children at Time 1 was black
(42 percent), followed by Puerto Ricans (31 percent) and "whites and
others" (27 percent). At Time 2, there was again no significant change in
these proportions but at Time 3 and Time 4, white children in general—
and Jewish children in particular—were discharged in significantly higher
proportions while black children were the ones least likely to be discharged. The final sample was 48 percent black, 36 percent Puerto
Rican, and 16 percent white.

Of the children in the original sample, 59 percent were Catholic, 35
percent Protestant, and 6 percent "Jewish and others." By the final year
of the study, the proportion of Catholics was slightly lower (56 percent),
the proportion of Protestants had increased (41 percent) while the minority of "Jewish and others" was reduced by half (3 percent). Since most
blacks are Protestant and most Puerto Ricans are Catholics, analyses involving religion and ethnicity nearly always produced the same findings.

Health

The large majority (72 percent) of the children were reported by the
workers to be in good health at Time 1. Common health problems—
such as childhood diseases, mild infections, the need for glasses—were
reported for 16 percent. For 9 percent, more significant health problems
(such as asthma) were named, but these were usually being treated and
were not necessarily a major obstacle in placement decisions. Major
health problems that did play a significant part in placement decisions
were reported for 3 percent of the children. Of these, most were severe

congenital disorders or developmental anomalies in infants and young children.

At Time 2, the proportion of children described as in good health dropped to 63 percent, but this most likely reflects the more detailed knowledge of common problems that workers acquired after the crisis period, rather than an actual increase in health problems among the children. At Time 3, the proportion of children free of health problems was 70 percent; at Time 4 it rose to 78 percent.

Development or Intelligence

Workers assigned to infants and preschool children were asked to describe the child's development; those reporting on older children were asked to give intelligence test scores, if these were known, or their impressions of the child's capacities. The results were similar to the picture obtained of the health status of the children. In 4 percent of the cases workers reported signs of serious developmental problems or an intelligence quotient below 80; in 11 percent, mild retardation was apparent or suspected or a test score in the "dull normal" category was reported; in 16 percent, workers reported test scores over 110 or their impression that the child's development was ahead of his age level. For the remaining 69 percent, development or intelligence was reported as normal or average.

Over time, this picture remained basically unchanged. At each cycle, the large majority of children were seen as normal. For 55 to 60 percent of the sample, the workers' impressions remained the same at successive points in time. In those cases where workers changed their opinion, the number of those who apparently improved was approximately equal to the number of those who apparently declined. All but a few of these changes represent differences of one step on the scale; major changes, either positive or negative, occurred only occasionally.

Emotional Problems

At Time 1, 36 percent of the children were described as well-adjusted throughout the period they had been known to the worker. An additional 14 percent had shown some signs of disturbance initially but were doing well at the time of the interview, while 18 percent continued to show some signs of disturbance, although it was anticipated that these could be dealt with in the normal course of the placement experience and did not constitute major problems. In 10 percent of the cases the children had been regarded as very disturbed at the time of initial placement but were no longer major problems, while another 10 percent had been regarded as very disturbed at the time of placement but were beginning to show signs of improvement. Twelve percent were reported as having serious disturbances, which were manifested during the entire period of placement.

Between Times 1 and 2, 51 percent of the children were evaluated as unchanged. Those described as worse slightly outnumbered those described as having improved, but again, the workers' greater knowledge of the child may account for this difference. Between Times 2 and 3, the number of those who improved was slightly higher than the number of those who were seen as having more problems. At the last time cycle, these differences were insignificant.

If one looked only at the children believed to have relatively serious problems, those who improved outnumbered those who deteriorated at both Time 2 and Time 3, but the situation was reversed between Time 3 and Time 4. At the last comparison, those whose emotional state was described as worse were more than double the number of those who improved. This may represent the combined effects of selectivity over time (the relatively healthy children were more likely to have gone home), of replacements, of continuing instability in the family, and of the onset of adolescence.

School Problems

The initial picture of the relative "normality" of children going into placement was altered somewhat when the workers' reports on their initial school status were considered. Of the 261 school-age children for whom reports were obtained at Time 1, 14 percent were described as having serious difficulties in school, in the form of chronic behavior problems or poor performance or both; 30 percent were reported as having difficulty of a less serious nature; 35 percent were said to be having no difficulty in school, and to be performing at their grade level, while an additional 21 percent were said to be "doing well" or working at an above average level. Thus nearly half the children who had reached school age at the time of placement were having some difficulty in school just before or during the early phases of placement.

At each of the subsequent cycles, the proportion of children having difficulty in school was slightly lower than at the time of the initial measure. An analysis of how this variable changed over time indicated that while 40 percent of the children were reported to have improved, only 19 percent were reported as worse. Between Times 2 and 3, there was little difference in direction, but between Times 3 and 4 the proportion of those who improved was again higher (32 percent) than the proportion of those for whom a decline was seen (27 percent). In other words, children placed at school age tended to have school difficulties, but over time they were more likely to improve in this area—at least in the eyes of their workers—than to deteriorate.

"Child Appeal"

Some of the observations made by the research staff at agency meetings during the planning period, as well as the dictates of common sense, suggested the presence of an intangible quality which, for lack of more precise terminology, was called "appeal," a characteristic some children seemed to possess independently of intelligence, physical attractiveness, or emotional disturbances. This factor seemed to contribute to their ability to attract attention to themselves, a skill anticipated as having a potentially important effect on the course of placement.

Workers were asked two questions: how appealing they thought the child was in general, and how they thought he appealed to the people caring for him and to the worker herself; it had been thought that a single question might produce a stereotyped response from child welfare workers predisposed to consider all children appealing or at least to refrain from identifying a child as "unappealing."

While workers did tend to answer all three questions affirmatively, the frequency distributions on each question differ somewhat, indicating that workers distinguished to some extent between their own subjective response to the child and the reactions of others. Table 4.1 reflects these differences.

The principal difference in these distributions, as is apparent from this table, was the workers' tendency to report children as "exceptionally appealing" to themselves more than to others. The obvious explanation is that workers were more aware of strong feelings in themselves, and had relatively less awareness, at least at this stage of placement, of how children affect others.

Since the small group of children identified early as "unappealing" seemed to be headed for a problematic future in foster care, the data were reviewed to determine what factors were associated with this lack of appeal. For half the cases reviewed, it was clear that such a deficiency was equated with uncommunicativeness. Occasionally, severe physical anomalies strained the worker's capacity to respond to the child, as did such traits as whining, hyperactivity, or manipulativeness; but failure to respond or relate to adults was far more conspicuous among the reasons for lack of appeal. Children described as unappealing to counselors or foster parents but particularly appealing to the worker were characterized by aggressive behavior which strained their relations with their caretakers;

TABLE 4.1

Child Appeal Ratings (in percentages) During the First Year of Placement
(N = 616)

	In General	To Child-Caring Persons	To Worker
Exceptionally appealing	12	16	32
Generally appealing	64	58	47
Average/mixed	18	19	16
Unappealing	6	7	5
	100	100	100

they nevertheless related to their workers and could therefore be counted as a "success" in treatment. The following case illustrates:

> An 11-year-old boy was placed in an institutional shelter; he was described as sullen, angry, and ready to strike out at anyone. Counselors felt he was impossible; others got tired of trying to help him. However, he came to the worker to complain about the institution and began to talk. She succeeded in establishing a relationship with the child, and reported some positive behavioral changes. She found him appealing because "he was a challenge." The interviewer, commenting that "challenge" seemed to her an understatement, noted that "It doesn't begin to express this worker's warm feeling for this child. She had obvious pride in the changes in his behavior and the closeness of their relationship."

Over time, for all three measures used, the picture remained consistent: Children who had evoked a favorable response continued to evoke one from other workers, as well as from those who knew them in their first year in placement. The proportion of children who elicited negative reactions diminished to 5 percent by the final cycle. The analysis of change over time indicated that those who evoke unfavorable reactions did so only once; only four children were described as "unappealing" at more than one point in time. Thus the child's "appeal" did not seem to play a significant role in his experience in placement.

Children's Reactions to Placement

Of the children old enough (over two) to have some awareness of the events in their lives, most were reported as adjusting well regardless of whether they had just been transferred to long-term care, had been in long-term care for some time, or had returned home. Not surprisingly, a higher proportion of children who had returned home (67 percent) were reported as reacting well to the change than those who had entered long-term care (52 percent).

The exception to this picture of generally positive reactions to placement status was that of the child's attitude toward interim care. Of 91 children in temporary settings, the majority (68 percent) were reported as unaware of or giving no indication of concern about their placement status. The next largest group (17 percent) were reported as either actively hostile to placement or having mixed feelings. About 15 percent were reported as accepting placement but indicating that they would rather be at home. Only two children were reported as wanting to remain in the temporary setting and none were reported to be looking forward to a new placement. Many of those in the unaware or no concern category may be there because they lacked a close relationship with their workers, but since the workers were generally knowledgeable about these children, it seems reasonable to infer that there was also much concealment of feeling among children whose status is "temporary."

Between Times 1 and 2, the proportion of children whose attitude toward placement became more positive was considerably higher (40 percent) than that of those who had become more negative (13 percent). Between Time 2 and Time 3, the proportion of negative change increased (27 percent) to the point where it nearly equaled changes for the better (32 percent). For the final comparison, the picture was again one of continuing acceptance (50 percent) and changes for the better (34 percent), but relatively little deterioration (16 percent).

As was noted in chapter 3, most of the problems described as associated with particularly difficult placements centered on the family or the agency. The child himself was the source of a major placement problem much less frequently. Where the child presented either a major or a secondary problem at Time 1, it was most often medical or developmental. Almost as frequently, the problem was a severe emotional disturbance which created special problems in handling. Least frequent were specific racial problems, such as color matching or mixed racial background, which made the child more than usually difficult to place.

Over time, the medical problems diminished in significance while emotional disturbance became more important. Racial problems were noted even less frequently in the later stages of placement than they were originally.

Summary

Despite the crises which bring them into placement, most children in care were initially perceived as healthy, developing normally, and relatively free of major emotional disturbance. Over time, the general picture of good health and normal development remained stable for the first four years. After the fourth year, however, the emotional stability of the children in the residual sample seemed more likely to deteriorate than to improve. It is possible that the initial picture underestimated the degree of disturbance, but the factors that lead to underestimation—worker pressures and other limitations—were substantially corrected by Time 2. Nevertheless, signs of increased emotional strain did not begin to appear until Time 4. Most children were apparently resilient enough—at least in the eyes of their workers—to come through both the crises which precipitated placement and a placement experience of several years. After three to four years, the combination of the onset of adolescence, the continued failures of the natural family, and the necessity of replacement for some may well be more strain than children can successfully tolerate.

Children who entered placement at school age tended to have a history of school difficulties, but over the time span of the study, they were seen as improving. Children considered "appealing" tended to remain so in the eyes of workers. Responses to long-term placement were generally seen as accepting, but reactions to returning home were more frequently positive. With children in interim placement, feelings seemed to be concealed or unclear to the workers.

The composite picture of the study children contrasts strikingly with that of the family. Most of the children were initially seen in favorable terms and these become increasingly positive over time. Most of the parents were initially seen in mixed or negative terms and these become increasingly negative over time. Up to a point, this difference seems inevitable. The children could readily be seen as victims; only a few had developed or were in the process of developing behavior of a socially troublesome nature. Their parents, in many instances, were involved in unacceptable forms of social behavior; and while many of their workers undoubtedly saw them as victims too, compassionate feelings for parents were clearly more difficult to sustain. Whatever the causes, the study data indicated that natural families were increasingly "out" of the system. Unless certain positive agency factors and certain family factors favored their return home, as will be seen in later chapters, children were increasingly "absorbed" in the system, although not necessarily increasingly comfortable in it.

chapter five

PLACEMENT: STRAINS AND PROBLEMS

T HE DATA PRESENTED in the discussion of the characteristics of three principal groups within the child welfare network—workers, families, and children—make evident the strains and problems in these relationships. Now, we shall consider some additional features of the placement situation, including an examination of some worker assessments of the problems presented.

The Placement Situation

At Time 1, when most study children had been in placement between six and nine months, nearly half (47 percent) had gone into long-term settings. One-third were still in temporary settings, while the remaining 20 percent had been discharged. Thus, in a system that formally defines a "temporary" placement as one of three months' duration or less, a third of the children in the study were still living in the vacuum of temporary settings after a period at least twice as long as the "official" time had elapsed.

The setting

Of the total Time 1 sample, a larger proportion of children in long-term care were in institutions than in foster homes. By Time 2, however, when nearly all the sample was in long-term care, the proportion in foster homes was higher than those in institutions. This difference increased in magnitude at Time 3, and by the final cycle, 62 percent of the study children were in long-term foster homes, and 25 percent in institutions. This difference reflects a number of factors: the general professional preference for foster homes, the use of foster homes as alternatives for children who do not do well in institutional care, the older age range of institutional children (which leads them to be discharged sooner than the younger children in foster homes), and the inclusion in the institutional sample of residential treatment centers, where discharge is expected after a two- to three-year stay.

At Time 1, the study children were placed with 61 child-caring agencies. It is instructive to note that although selection of the sample took nine months, 12 of the eligible agencies evidently had so little turnover that they did not take even one study child during that time.

Of those who were involved in the study, 35 agencies had five or fewer children in the study at Time 1, 21 had between six and twenty study children, while only 5 agencies took more than twenty-one children. The Time 2 pattern was similar, but in the two later cycles of the study the sample was even more dispersed because two-thirds of the agencies had five or fewer children in the study. At Time 4, only two agencies had more than 21 children.

Foster families

At Time 1, the foster parents were about evenly divided between those who were relatively experienced (having cared for at least three foster children other than the study subjects) and those having cared for two or fewer. At Time 2, the proportion of "experienced" foster parents rose to 55 percent, then declined to the earlier level at later phases.

Workers were asked to rate the foster parents on a three-point scale ranging from "acceptable" to "highly valued." As would be expected, the response was heavily skewed in favor of the more positive evaluations. At Time 1, however, 26 percent of the foster homes fell into the "acceptable" category (able to serve as foster homes in selected cases or for emergencies although they had, in the eyes of their workers, serious limitations). At Time 2, when most of the homes were involved in long-term care and were assessed by higher standards, workers had reservations for about one in three, but most of these doubts were overshadowed by the positive factors in the home. More serious reservations indicating the possibility of replacement for the study child were described for 12 percent of the foster homes at Time 2, 15 percent at Time 3 but, with an increasingly stabilized sample, the proportion dropped to 7 percent at Time 4.

The most common form of praise for the foster parent was for warmth, concern, and "extra" attention given the child—a pattern which was consistent throughout the four cycles. From Time 2 on, the next most common positive factor seen in the foster homes was the treatment of the foster child as "one of the family," often with a potential for adoption.

Reasons for negative evaluations were more varied and changed over time. At Time 1, the limitation most frequently mentioned was the foster mother's ability to care only for specific types of children: infants, children in need of temporary care, those free of emotional disturbance, etc. Second most frequent were complaints about rigidity and excessive demands for conformity. Financial motivation was also mentioned but usually in conjunction with other drawbacks.

At Time 2, the foster homes' limited ability to handle either younger or older children or children with special problems continued to be a major reason for a negative evaluation by the worker, but it lost significance in the two later cycles, when the child sample no longer included infants and the children were more stabilized in placement.

From Time 2 on, the dominant reason for worker doubts about foster homes, appearing in over a third of the 100 cases reviewed in a content analysis, centered on the foster mother's inability to strike the desired balance between permissiveness and control. They were described as either too strict, rigid, or punitive, or at the other extreme, too permissive, unable to discipline, overprotective, or overindulgent. At Times 2 and 3, the overly permissive foster mother was described more frequently than the rigid one; at the final cycle, the two extremes were described with equal frequency.

It is also worth noting that when all reasons—major and minor—for negative evaluations were listed, the one named most frequently was strained relationships with the natural parents; but this usually appeared as a secondary problem. Other problems which were specific to the foster parent role (such as financial motivations, difficulty in relating to agency workers, and failures to cooperate with agency procedures) were mentioned fairly frequently. There were also occasional complaints that the children were not sufficiently stimulated or that there was little interest in schooling.

The overriding impression, however, was that the major problems lay in the quality of the foster mother's mothering—problems that may be no different from those of other mothers, but that confront the worker and the agency with the question of how much guidance is needed and whether and at what point removal is warranted. Only a few cases were described in which the agency had a clear case for removal or termination of the home.

The following cases illustrate a number of the problems mentioned:

> *Time 1:* Foster mother seems to prefer babies under a year old and she becomes very involved with them. . . . Informant is beginning to wonder whether foster mother is not better for babies than for children who are subject's age . . . feels that she may not be giving him sufficient stimulation . . . children may spend too much time watching TV.
>
> *Time 2:* Foster mother is very accepting of the children but the general emotional and social atmosphere of the home is very rigid and restrictive. . . . She stresses academic achievement above social adjustment, tends to discourage friendships and activities outside the home. . . . She does give them good physical care. Worker foresees many problems if subject and sibling are raised in this home. . . . However, they are happy and secure here.
>
> *Time 3:* Foster parents are very positive and loving. Foster mother tends to be overprotective and especially cautious in relation to health. They can't handle acting out at all and are very threatened by it. . . . They favor subject over the sibling because he is more docile and conforming. They couldn't handle another older sibling at all and he had to be placed in another foster home, but they have a positive feeling toward him and encourage their foster children to maintain a close relationship with him. . . . They will find it difficult to cope with adolescence, but they care a great deal, try hard, and seem amenable to help.
>
> *Time 4:* Foster family is quite accepting of subject. They include her in decision making but have had conflicts over household responsibilities. She loves natural child and is very motherly toward another foster child in the home. . . . Foster mother is temperamental and subject to mood swings. She feels she is so competent she can't take suggestions from anyone, including the agency. She is rigid and lacks openness . . . but this is a satisfactory placement for child because home has many positives, especially foster father, who is warm, understanding, giving person.

Institutional settings

As was the case with the foster parents, the relatively broad range of topics necessarily covered by the interview limited the number of questions that could be asked. At Time 1, it was assumed that the experience of the counselors and the workers' evaluation of their abilities would serve as an indicator, equivalent to the foster parents' experience and the workers' evaluation of their abilities. The frequencies obtained at Time 1 indicated that most counselors (68 percent) had three years or more of experience and almost as great a proportion (64 percent) were rated as highly valued. The rating given and the number of years of experience were fairly closely related. The figures obtained, however, were considered dubious for a number of reasons. Many workers were very vague in their answers and indicated that their knowledge of the counseling staff was minimal. While social workers are expected to evaluate foster mothers, many thought it inappropriate to pass judgment on fellow staff members. There was a particular reluctance in Catholic institutions, where the worker is a lay person and the house mother a member of a religious order.

In the later cycles of the study, other data describing the institutional program were collected in an effort to find a reliable indicator of the quality of care within the limitations of the study. This was only partially successful, probably because the agency phase of the study depended entirely on data that caseworkers could provide. The latter were not directly involved in institutional programs.

The measure of institutional care that was relatively productive was the extent to which the child was reported to be attracting attention of a nonroutine nature. Most of this attention was apparently based on negative rather than positive factors; children attracted attention to themselves by provocative or other problematic behavior, rather than through their attractiveness, abilities, or capacities for leadership. The analysis indicated that the most disturbed children drew attention to themselves significantly more often than did the less disturbed. In the later phases of the study, the proportion of disturbed children receiving special attention from the staff increased markedly. The staff's ability to respond, whether provoked or not, could be seen as a criterion of service if one assumed that the disturbed child should receive more attention than those more nearly "normal."

At Time 1, the proportion of children reported to be receiving more than routine attention from counseling staff was 20 percent. At Time 2, this proportion rose to 35 percent, and by the time of the final cycle of data collection half the children in institutional care were said to be receiving such attention. The greatest change for the better took place between Times 1 and 2. The later changes were in the same direction but not so strong.

Evaluating the Placement Situation

Workers were asked several questions which constituted an evaluation of the placement situation, such as whether the placement was in the child's best interests, how long he would be likely to need care, whether the parents were likely to remain in contact, as well as questions about inter- and intra-agency problems associated with placement.

Not surprisingly, the large majority of Time 1 workers, who were obviously the ones closest to the actual decision, thought the placement absolutely or very necessary; but for 13 percent, workers had some doubts and in some cases thought the placement clearly unnecessary. This proportion dropped to 6 percent by Time 2.

At Time 3, the question was adapted to the perspective of workers who were several years removed in time from the events that precipitated placement. They were asked whether they saw, in retrospect, any way that placement might have been prevented. Workers expressed doubts about the validity of the original placement decision for 20 percent of the children still in placement at Time 3 and 17 percent of those still in placement at Time 4.

In comparing the responses of the workers at Times 1 and 2, it was found that for 85 percent of the children, both workers consistently judged the placement to be necessary. Time 3 workers upheld the initial confirmation of the need for placement for 73 percent of the children still in care, Time 4 workers for care for 77 percent.

The analysis indicated that the most common reasons for changes in the assessment of need for placement were evidence that the pathology in the parent was more severe than had originally been thought or that the interest or capacity of relatives to help had been overestimated. Cases where the assessment was upward were often characterized by the fact that the Time 2 worker was more removed from the initial events and lacked some knowledge that the original worker had.

In comparing the evaluations of need made by the workers assigned to the later phases of placement, it was found that workers were consistent in their assessment that placement might have been prevented in only 14 cases, and had disagreed in 70 cases. The lack of casework help at the time of the crisis or at later stages was the most commonly named problem in relation both to preventing placement and to shortening it.

Predicting future need

At each cycle, workers were asked to make predictions about the child's future in placement. At Time 1, predictions as to the chances that those children still in placement would return home were fairly evenly distributed along a six-point scale ranging from "no chance" to "strong chance." According to their workers, 30 percent of the children had a strong chance of returning to their families in less than a year. Of the children in interim care, the smallest proportion (24 percent) were expected to return home in less than a year. The remainder were almost evenly divided between those who the workers expected to remain in placement for several years and those who they thought would remain in care until they were adults. In later phases of the study, the proportion expected to return to their homes diminished, as would be expected, to 21 percent at Time 2, 16 percent at Time 3, and only 9 percent at the final cycle. Correspondingly, the proportion of children who workers felt would be in care until they were eighteen rose from 37 percent at Time 1 to 57 percent at Time 2, remained there at Time 3, and rose to 71 percent at Time 4. At each succeeding cycle, the worker sample became significantly more pessimistic, except for the Time 2–Time 3 comparison.

Of the children for whom adoption appeared at least a theoretical possibility in the sense that contact with parents was minimal, workers saw no chance at all for such an outcome for 60 percent, a slight chance for 19 percent, and a fair chance for 21 percent. This is not surprising; the study, because it limited its sample to children in placement three months or longer, excluded healthy white infants who were readily adoptable. The figures also reflect the general pessimism, prevalent when the study began, about adoption as an answer to the problems of any group of children other than healthy, white infants.

A review of the cases in which children were considered good candidates for adoption at Time 1 indicated that nearly all were infants under one year of age. In some instances, adoption was planned but complicated by medical or other problems, such as ambivalence on the mother's part. However, the most common situation, involving nearly half this group, was that in which the mother had been involved in some form of grossly deviant behavior such as severe neglect, continued abandonment, prostitution, drug addiction, or psychosis. Although the question of adoption had not been discussed with the mother, workers apparently thought, in view of the child's age and the mother's history, that adoption would eventually be considered.

The proportion of children for whom adoption was considered a possibility dropped to 4 percent at Time 2 but rose again to 20 percent at Time 3 and to 24 percent at Time 4. This increase in optimism parallels the changes in the New York adoption scene that took place during the later phases of the study. Laws permitting foster parents to obtain subsidies and adopt children who had been with them for some time went into effect. Nearly all the children considered "adoptable" in the later phases of the study were in stable foster homes, where the use of the subsidy was under consideration.

The validity of the predictions made—i.e., the extent to which the workers proved to be correct in their judgments—is discussed in chapter 7.

Agency strains [1]

As was indicated in chapters 3 and 4, each placement situation was analyzed in terms of the extent to which it was "problematic" to the agency. At Time 1, half the cases in the sample were seen as presenting major difficulties. Over time, the proportion of "problems," as would be expected, diminished to 31 percent at Time 2, 20 percent at Time 3, and 24 percent at Time 4—reflecting again the increased stabilization of the sample, as well as the fact that many of the most dissatisfied parents had succeeded in removing their children, and that in some instances the most disturbed children had been transferred to non–foster care settings such as state mental hospitals or institutions for the retarded.

Some of the problems described earlier originated with the family and some with the child, but a substantial number were inherent in the particular agency or in the relationships within or among agencies. Such agency-based problems complicated the placement situation in nearly half the cases.

Among the agency problems at Time 1, the most common were cat-

1. The problem of re-placement is reported in Eugene Shinn, *Placement Patterns: A Five-Year Analysis of Placement, Replacement and Discharge of CWRP Study Children* (New York: Columbia University School of Social Work, Child Welfare Research Project, 1972).

egorized as "bureaucratic delays," usually decisions requiring special consideration, such as those which had to be approved by higher levels of authority. They also involved differences of opinion between agencies which had to be resolved at higher levels. Failures or delays in obtaining necessary information were also common forms of interagency problems. Next in frequency came the lack of appropriate placements—i.e., available foster homes or institutional space were not suitable for the particular child or for him and his siblings. In only 7 percent of the cases was the problem identified as the lack of foster homes or institutional space in and of itself. Since emphasis in discussions of the need for placement is so often on deficiency in supply, it is particularly worth noting that problems centering on bureaucratic entanglements here outnumbered those which centered on sheer absence of resources.

In the later phases of the study, the proportion of cases considered "problematic" declined from 51 to 31 percent at Time 2, 20 percent at Time 3, and 24 percent at the final cycle. The major sources of the problem described—a combination of family and agency factors—did not apparently differ much from what the situation had been at Time 1. The nature of the agency problem, however, does seem to vary over time. Complaints about "bureaucratic delays" increased at Time 2 to 32 percent of those cases in which agency-based problems were reported. This proportion declined to 20 percent at Time 3 and finally to 10 percent at Time 4, reflecting again the more settled nature of the final sample. The frequency with which workers had difficulty in finding an "appropriate" placement fluctuated from one cycle to another, but over all did not seem to change significantly. The proportion of cases, however, where the problem was an internal one in the foster home rose from 2 percent at Time 1 to 31 percent at Time 4, reflecting the increased use of foster homes.

Multiple Agency Involvement

It was evident early that since children came into foster care at times of major family crises, the involvement of agencies other than those in the child welfare system were critical factors in placement. Workers were asked about the number of agencies active with the family, the nature of their involvement, and the problems, if any, associated with such involvement. "Involvement" was defined as having a connection with the problem that precipitated placement, or being part of the placement process itself.

The term "agencies" was defined broadly to include such social institutions as the police, the church, and the school system, as well as medical and psychiatric clinics and hospitals, public assistance, children's services, and family agencies. The findings indicate that such involvement was extensive during the first year. In only 4 percent of the cases were the agencies limited to the two required by the child welfare system. The median number of agencies involved per family was six while the upper end of the range was eighteen. Seven or more agencies were involved in over a third of the families. Even within the child welfare network, the degree of agency involvement was high. Fifty-seven percent of the families were known to at least one other child welfare agency in addition to the intake agency and the agency caring for the study subject.

Not surprisingly, the agency most commonly involved with the study families was public assistance, which was active to some degree in 52 percent of the cases. Medical clinics and hospitals were named in 48 percent of the cases while psychiatric settings were involved in 43 percent. Among the less involved agencies were those offering services to children in the home (child guidance clinics, school programs, day-care centers, etc.), which were active in 30 percent of the cases; family agencies were active in 21 percent, legal agencies (criminal courts, prisons, legal aid societies), in 20 percent, and poverty programs in 6 percent.

After Time 1, the involvement of other agencies declined markedly. The median number of agencies involved was three at Time 2; the same held true for Time 3. By Time 4, the median was two, which meant that for half the children in care, the agency represented by the worker interviewed was the only one currently active, at least to that worker's knowledge.

At all points in time, public assistance remains the principal agency involved, but the proportion of cases dropped to 40 percent at Time 2. The proportion involved with medical or psychiatric agencies was reduced by half in the later phases of the study while the involvement of other types of agencies continued to be negligible.

The changes in part reflect the passing of the crisis period that precipitated the placement, but they also reflected the declining involvement of the agency with the family. It is entirely possible that many families were receiving service not known to the worker, but this does not alter the fact that, by the fifth year, services of non–child welfare agencies were not a significant factor in the care of most children, as far as the agency responsible was concerned.

Internal Professional Involvement

For more than two-thirds of the children, no members of the agency's professional staff other than social workers were involved in direct, individual contact with them or their families in the first year of placement. Twenty-eight percent had either a psychological test, a psychiatric examination, medical attention other than routine physicals, or some combination of these services. The proportion receiving such attention increased to 33 percent at Time 2, 41 percent at Time 3, and 37 percent at Time 4. In all, 61 percent of the children received professional attention from someone other than a social worker over the five-year period.

Since not every child is equally in need of specialized help, it is difficult to gauge the extent to which these figures approach an adequate investment for the agency system. Its probable inadequacy is suggested by the workers' report, at Time 2, that 46 percent of the children had some need for service in addition to what the placement situation was giving them. Of those with unmet needs, 57 percent were in the area of individual therapy. At each of the two successive cycles, the proportion of those with unmet needs rose—to 55 percent at Time 3 and 58 percent at Time 4. The proportion of those specifically in need of individual therapy rose to 63 percent at the final cycle. In their final assessment, workers considered the casework service given as inadequate for fully half the children. They also expressed the opinion that the service given had been consistently poor over the entire period for 20 percent.

Final Assessments

At each point, workers were asked to evaluate the effect of placement on the child and on the family for those who had been discharged. At the final cycle, workers were asked an additional series of evaluative questions about all the children expected to remain in care.

At Time 1, 21 percent of the discharges which occurred during that period were described as dubious (i.e., seen as objectionable by at least one of the workers involved in the decision). This proportion reached 27 percent at Time 2, declined to 24 percent at Time 3, and to 17 percent at the final cycle.

At Time 2, workers expressed the opinion that placement had been harmful or had mixed effects on the child for 24 percent of those discharged. This proportion rose to 33 percent at Time 3, and 37 percent at Time 4. The most commonly named negative effect was increasing fearfulness and anxiety. Effects on the mother were described as negative for 32 percent at Time 2, 31 percent at Time 3, and 26 percent at Time 4. The most commonly named negative effects were extreme guilt feelings and the threat of loss of the children.

In the final assessment of the residual sample, workers thought that the placement experience of the child had damaged the sense of self-worth for 23 percent and the capacity to trust adults for 20 percent. They expressed concern for the future of 26 percent, and anticipated school problems for 30 percent of the younger children and occupational problems for 32 percent of the older ones.

Summary and Discussion

Study children were largely absorbed by the long-term agencies by the second year of the study. The initial use of institutional settings was superseded by the use of foster homes in the later stages of the study.

The foster homes used were about evenly divided between those caring for at least three other children and those who were less experienced. In the early stages of placement, workers had reservations about the quality of care given by every third or fourth foster home. These reservations diminished over time. The major problem workers dealt with in relation to foster homes paralleled the agency problems with the natural mother mentioned in chapter 3: determination of whether the quality of the foster mother's care was adequate.

The quality of care given by institutional workers was more difficult to assess. The figures indicated that the staff was increasingly able to individualize demands for attention, usually from relatively disturbed children.

The large majority of placements were consistently seen as essential by most of the workers involved. Where doubts were expressed about the validity of the placement decision, it was usually by only one worker of the several interviewed.

Nearly half the children were expected to return home during the initial year of placement. By the final year, most were expected to remain in care until 18. Slightly offsetting this expectation was an increase in optimism about the possibility of adoption.

Initially, about half the cases in care involved major agency-centered problems, a proportion which is reduced by half over the time of the study. The major agency-centered problems were described as "bureaucratic delays," prevalent for the first two years after placement, after which problems in the foster home become more prominent.

Involvement in the broad network of agencies was high in the first year but declined sharply by the second year, after which interaction with other agencies was negligible.

At all times, about a third of the sample received some form of special professional attention but the figures produced by workers' statements of unmet needs suggested that this was far from adequate.

In summarizing the impact of placement, most discharges were described as planned and by agreement among the parties concerned. Most children and families were seen as benefiting by the experience, or at the very least not harmed by it.

The principal question here is whether the "failure" rate suggested by the indicators used in the study is tolerable. No service system of any kind expects total success, but it is obliged to keep the failure rate as low as possible. In the system under scrutiny, the workers' reports indicated that every fourth discharge was questioned, that one child in four of those who remained in the system for five years was seen as harmed by the placement experience. Every third or fourth mother of these children was seen as having experienced more harm than good from the placement experience. One child in four was seen as having suffered damaged self-esteem. For one child in three, workers felt that they had cause to be anxious for their future, either in school or as adults. The system was apparently seen as beneficial largely to those who left it relatively early.

When one combines the key data reported in this and the preceding chapter, a portrait emerges of a system of services which can best be characterized as a necessary evil—one that becomes increasingly ingrown, drifts away from the family and other community resources, while professional concern increasingly focuses on children and foster mothers. The quality of that concern improves and the children may receive better service over time. Nevertheless, two-thirds of the children returned home within the five-year span of the period; many were perceived as improved in a number of ways by their experiences, and the same could be said for some families. What factors within the system contributed to such favorable outcomes? What differentiated the children who went home from those who remained in care with respect to the services they had received from the agency? Did a higher investment of worker training and experience make a difference? How heavily did a favorable or an unfavorable evaluation on the part of a worker count in determining whether a child continued in foster care? Answers to these and related questions will be the subject of the next two chapters.

PART TWO

INVESTMENT AND OUTCOME

chapter six

SERVICE ASSETS AND OUTCOMES

THE DESCRIPTION of the study's design in chapter 1 indicated that the concept of investment was developed into a series of measures that reflected some of the conditions under which services were given. Of these, four were relatively objective, quantifiable measures: the degree of contact with the child and the family and with others on their behalf, the worker's training and experience, the size of the worker's case load, and the worker's stability.[1]

These four measures were collectively called "service assets," and in effect reflect assumptions common to social work practice in general. Ever since social work entered its period of professionalization, half a century ago, it has been assumed that low case loads are better than high case loads, that the more experienced and trained the worker is, and that the more attention given the client the more favorable the outcome for him—whatever the goal of the service may be. The design of this study made it possible to examine these assumptions in relation to three outcomes: discharge from foster care, improvement in the child while in care, and improvement in the family, at least as seen by the worker.

Outcome Measures

The outcome variables for the study could be defined in several ways as was indicated in chapter 1. The most basic is the location of the child at

1. Most of the findings in this chapter were reported in two papers: "Agency Investment in Foster Care: A Study," *Social Work* 17, No. 4 (July 1972): 20–28; and "Agency Investment in Foster Care: After the First Year," *Social Work* 18, No. 6 (November 1973): pp. 3–9.

the end of the five-year period of the study: whether he was at home (natural or adoptive) or remained in long-term placement. In terms of the commonly accepted values of the child welfare system, the child's return home to conditions that are in some way better than they were at his placement was the most desirable outcome. For those who had to remain in long-term placement, a stable situation in either a foster home or an institution was at least a lesser evil than the frequent shifts of foster care settings to which many children are subjected. Thus, one could rank the outcomes from greatest to least desirability as follows:

1. Discharge home under conditions defined as desirable by those concerned.
2. Stable long-term placement.
3. Discharge to an unimproved natural family situation.
4. Unstable long-term placement.

The various forms of investment could then be related to each of the categories of outcome to determine which, if any, had significant influence in either a favorable or an unfavorable direction. Within the framework of this study, outcome could also be defined as the extent to which the child or the family improved during the period designated, either as determined by objective measures such as changes in the test scores or behavior ratings or through the judgments made by workers and other appropriate staff.

For each of the four study cycles, the children who continued in care were compared to those who returned home. At Time 1, it was possible to contrast the children in interim care with those who returned home early in placement and those for whom long-term placement had already been decided upon and achieved. At each point, there were an insufficient number of children who were discharged against the advice or better judgment of agency personnel to be treated separately in the analysis. Thus, the "discharged" group consists mainly of children who were discharged by design. Similarly, there were an insufficient number of children who changed placements within each time cycle to be treated separately. Thus the "in care" group consists mainly of children who remained in the same placement during the time cycle covered.[2] For

2. The impact of repeated placements on children as measured by psychological tests is discussed in David Fanshel and Eugene B. Shinn, *Children in Foster Care* (New York: Columbia University Press, forthcoming).

purposes of analyses then, categories 1 and 3 of the outcomes listed were combined, as were categories 2 and 4.

The degree of improvement in the child at Time 1 was judged by the coding staff on the basis of the data given by the worker best acquainted with the child. The degree of improvement in the family was also judged by the coding staff on the basis of the data given by the worker best acquainted with the family. "Improvement" was defined as any description by the worker of a visible change for the better—such as a modification of the child's or the family's attitudes (making them more accessible to involvement with the worker) or a move to better housing or a better job, a recovery from an illness, or a greater acceptance of separation.[3]

From Time 2 on, the measure of improvement in the child was an index composed of several different statements made by the worker, reflecting improvement in various areas. However, attrition in the sample size and the reduction in involvement made it difficult to obtain a similar index for improvement in the family. The measure used was an evaluation by the worker, which was placed on a five-point scale ranging from "marked deterioration" to "marked improvement." These terms referred only to the mother—so often the family member best known to the agency.

Outcome Frequencies

Discharge

The frequency distributions obtained for discharge at Time 1 indicated that, at the time of data collection, when most of the children had been in care from six to nine months, not quite half (47 percent) were in long-term placement. One-third were still in temporary settings while the remaining 20 percent had already been discharged. Of those in temporary care, the large majority were awaiting long-term placement and the rest were about evenly divided between those waiting to be sent home and those for whom plans were undecided.

By Time 2, 73 percent of the children were in long-term settings; only 5 percent remained in the temporary shelter of boarding homes. At Time 1, 20 percent of the original sample had been discharged, and by Time 2,

3. The relationship between agency investment as reflected by the "service assets" described in this chapter and improvement as measured by changes in intelligence and psychological tests is also discussed in the Fanshel and Shinn volume.

another 22 percent of those remaining in care were released. At Time 3, the discharge figure was 28 percent, and at Time 4, 20 percent. Since the time intervals between each measure were not equal, these differences do not reflect the overall rate of change. More precise figures [4] for yearly intervals indicated that the discharge rate for the first year was relatively high (28 percent), but leveled off afterward—varying from 14 to 18 percent of the children remaining in care for each of the four remaining years of the study.

From the standpoint of the agency goal of returning children to their own families or placing them for adoption (also seen as a form of discharge), it seems clear that the possibilities are maximal in the first year but it is also important to note that they do not disappear in the next four years, so that the children are not necessarily "locked" into placement for the rest of childhood. It is worth noting that, at the time of the final interview, workers still saw at least a fair chance for discharge for 28 percent of the remaining children.

Improvement in the child

Nine percent of the children were judged to have shown marked improvement—i.e., in more than one area of functioning—during the time that had elapsed since placement. For 42 percent, some improvement was seen, most commonly an adjustment to the placement situation itself, while 28 percent were assessed by the worker as having always been in satisfactory condition and to have maintained their ability to function well during placement. The remaining 21 percent were those for whom no changes were reported by the worker. In general, the initial sample was about evenly divided between children known to have improved in the first year of placement and those who apparently did not, at least as far as was known to their worker.

At Time 2, the proportion of children reported as improved dropped slightly to 45 percent. In the two later cycles of data collection, the proportion of those who had improved came closer to two-thirds: 67 percent at Time 2 and 62 percent at the final measure.

Improvement in the family

At Time 1, the family situation was judged to be the same as at the time of placement in 56 percent of the cases. For 6 percent, the picture was

4. These are based on data collected by Dr. Eugene B. Shinn.

mixed: improvement was seen in some instances but there was also a lack of improvement or deterioration in others. For 31 percent, one indication of improvement was given but in only 7 percent was there more than one. Thus the Time 1 family sample was divided between approximately 60 percent unimproved and 40 percent improved.

The proportion of cases where improvement was reported in the mother was one-third at Time 2 and remained at that level throughout the five-year period. This is somewhat surprising, since one would expect the residual families of the children who spent all five years in placement to present a more discouraging picture than the initial family sample does. This may mean that workers saw improvement in such areas as acceptance of placement, ways of relating to their children, etc., but not, as was noted in chapter 4, in their capacity to assume responsibility for their children.

Service assets: frequencies
As was indicated in chapter 2, the majority of workers at all four cycles had only a BA degree. The proportion of fully trained workers, however, rose from 17 percent at Time 1 to 25 percent at Time 4. Their work experience was typically two years. The median case load at Time 1 was 36 but it dropped to 25 at Time 2 and remained at that level for the rest of the study.

Measures of the intensity of contact centering around the child or the family were produced by a more complex computation. At each cycle, workers were asked to list in chronological order or to summarize the number of activities they had engaged in for each case: interviews, home visits, supervisory conferences, contacts with other agencies, etc. These were averaged for the period in care. A correlational analysis indicated that most forms of activity varied together systematically, which made possible two indices: one reflected the degree of contact centered on the family, the other, the degree of contact centered on the child.

The first index was a combination of five items: (1) the number of office interviews, home visits and telephone calls to the parents; (2) contacts with other agencies; (3) supervisory conferences; (4) contacts with collateral; (5) the number of letters or reports. The second index was a combination of three items: (1) contacts with the child; (2) visits to the child-caring persons; (3) contacts with specialists such as psychologists or psychotherapists. Both indices demonstrated that the investment in the typical case at Time 1 was an average of one action a month, either directed to the client or concerning the client. The highest investment group was composed of those where action of some type was taken at least twice a month. As might be expected, only the children in institutions for the emotionally disturbed received attention along the lines of the traditional clinical model of regular weekly appointments. Thus the investment of actual time and effort per child and family is not high by many social work standards, but the range was broad enough so that five categories of worker attention to children and families might be distinguished: minimum worker attention, below average, average, above average, and maximum.

From Time 2 on, it was possible to use a single index to reflect time spent on the case, since most activity was vested in the same worker and the analysis indicated that frequency of contact with the family varied directly with frequency of contact with the child. After Time 1, changes in the pattern of case activity varied with the type of activity. High levels of activity in two areas—written reporting and contacts with collateral persons (interested persons in the community such as friends, neighbors, relatives other than parents or substitute parents)—tended to be characteristic of the first year only. After that, there was a net decline in such activity; the number of cases in which activity diminished was higher than the number in which it increased. Contact with other agencies declined after the first year, except for a small increment between Times 3 and 4.

Contact with parents also declined, but the sharpest change was between the first measure and the second. After that, the situation became relatively stable, since the number of families with whom contact was less frequent was only slightly greater than the number with whom contact had increased.

The frequency of direct contact with the children increased between Time 1 and Time 2, as would be expected with the movement of children from overcrowded, understaffed shelters to the better staffed long-term care agencies. After Time 2, such activity leveled off, with the largest proportion of children receiving the same degree of attention that they had been receiving earlier.

Contacts with foster parents or institutional staff followed a similar pattern: an increase after the first years, which subsequently leveled off. Contacts with supervisors and other interested staff members increased relatively more sharply between the first and second measures, continued to increase between the second and third, and then dropped sharply between the third and fourth measures, apparently as the children settled into seemingly permanent foster care.

At Time 1, 40 percent of the children in the study had experienced at least one change in workers even though they had been in placement less than a year; 54 percent of the children still in care had experienced such turnover at Time 2, 61 percent at Time 3, and 56 percent at Time 4. The difference between Time 1 and the subsequent measures does not necessarily represent a worsening situation, since the time periods covered by the later measures were longer, obviously permitting more turnover to take place. One can infer, however, that the situation with respect to worker stability is bad during the first year of placement and remains so throughout the five-year span of the study, despite the transfer of most of the children from the public to the voluntary system.

In general, the situation with respect to the service given the study sample was one of increased quality after the first year, as reflected in worker training and frequency of contact. Chances for discharge diminished while chances for improvement in the eyes of the workers increased for the child and remained stable for the family. It was possible that the "service assets" would all contribute to the discharges that took place as well as to the improvement seen. In fact, however, the findings indicate that the impact of the service assets diminished gradually over the span of the study, with little "payoff" five years after placement, especially with respect to discharge.

Other influential variables

It was evident in planning the analysis that other variables were also likely to influence each outcome at least as much as if not more than the "service assets" described. Discharge and improvement could obviously be a function of family characteristics or of variables describing the agency rather than the worker.

At each point, all independent variables were cross-tabulated with the status of the child and the judgments as to whether there had been improvement in the child and in his family. Those variables found to be statistically significant were then entered into a regression analysis in order to determine the extent to which they interacted, their relative influences on the outcome, and the degree of variance in the outcomes for which they accounted. These variables accounted for 19 percent of the variance in the child's status at Time 1, 20 percent at Time 2, 19 percent at Time 3, and 20 percent at Time 4. Nine percent of the variance in child improvement was accounted for at Time 1, but with the improved measures used in the later phases of the study, 17 percent was accounted for at Time 2, 12 percent at Time 3, and 32 percent at Time 4. Finally, 26 percent of the variance in improvement in the family was accounted for at Time 1, 30 percent at Time 2, 22 percent at Time 3, and 30 percent at Time 4.

At Times 1 and 2, "service assets" accounted for more of the variance on discharge than any other group of variables examined. At Times 3 and 4, however, client characteristics accounted for more of the variance, while service assets became relatively unimportant.

Improvement in the child as seen by the worker was closely related to other worker attitudes. After Time 1, certain client characteristics were closely associated with this form of outcome, and they continued to be at Time 3; but they diminished in importance at the final measure. Agency characteristics also contributed to this form of outcome—particularly at Time 2—while the service assets were significant only at Time 1.

The improvement perceived in the family was most closely associated with client characteristics at Time 1 but was also closely related to other worker attitudes. After Time 1, the influence of client characteristics became secondary, while the relationship to other worker attitudes become stronger. After Time 2, neither service assets nor other agency characteristics played a role in this form of outcome. The influence of client and organizational variables will be discussed in chapter 7.

Discharge and Service Assets

Worker experience

The hypothesis was that the probability of the child's continuing in placement would be lower if he had a trained, experienced worker. This hypothesis was partially upheld at Time 1 but not in the way that the division of function in this child welfare network would lead one to expect. As was indicated in chapter 1, one agency temporarily cared for the child while the public intake department of another worked with the family toward a decision whether to return the child home or place him on a long-term basis. It was therefore necessary to examine the influence of

TABLE 6.1

Status of the Child and Worker Experience at Time I [a]

	Family Sample—Planning Agencies (N = 272) [b,c]				Child Sample—Under-Care Agencies (N = 403) [b,d]			
Status	Least Experienced (N = 68)	Average (N = 50)	Above Average (N = 53)	Most Experienced (N = 101)	Least Experienced (N = 93)	Average (N = 79)	Above Average (N = 77)	Most Experienced (N = 154)
	%	%	%	%	%	%	%	%
At home	31	28	36	36	22	30	25	39
In long-term care	15	18	9	15	22	20	12	20
Undecided	10	8	6	7	10	13	10	8
Awaiting home	7	12	9	12	7	8	17	12
Awaiting long-term care	37	34	40	30	39	29	36	21
	100	100	100	100	100	100	100	100

[a] Two lowest categories of worker experience were combined because of small numbers.

[b] All tables exclude children in long-term placement where the worker interviewed represented the long-term care agency, since they did not participate actively in the placement situation. The children "in long-term care" represented in the table are those whose transfer took place shortly before the interview, for whom the worker in the interim care agency was the respondent. This also serves to eliminate those children who are readily absorbed by the network of long-term care agencies or those whose "waiting" period is relatively short.

[c] Chi-square = 5.176 with 12 df.; not significant.

[d] Chi-square = 23.088 with 12 df.; significant at .02 level.

the experience of family and child-care workers. When family workers' experience and training [2] were related to discharge, no significant difference was found. The number of children awaiting long-term care and assigned to the least experienced workers was only slightly higher than the number assigned to the most experienced workers; but when the experience of the workers at the child-caring agency was examined, the relationship between their experience and the children's status was statistically significant and in the expected direction. There were more than three times as many children awaiting long-term care in the case loads of the least experienced workers as there were for the most experienced. A considerably larger number of children who were cases of the most experienced workers returned home. It is also worth noting that the greatest differences occur between the most experienced group and all the others. Two to three years' experience made little difference; but five years or more, combined with some training, did.

At Time 2, worker experience showed no relationship to the discharges that took place then. At Time 3, this variable was again influential but interpretation was more complicated—this was the period in which more than half the children placed in residential treatment centers were discharged, and these agencies had the highest proportion of trained workers. To control this, the group in the highest scores on the index was left out of the analysis. With this control, it was observed that the group in the second-highest category of experience—those with partial training and considerable experience, who are proportionately distributed among the various types of agencies involved—still had a significantly higher proportion of discharges than did those with less training or experience.

TABLE 6.2

Discharge at Time 3 and Worker Experience (N = 313 *Children*) [a]

Status	Untrained; Inexperienced (N = 97) %	Untrained; Some Experience (N = 93) %	Partial Training; Some Experience (N = 58) %	Partial Training; Considerable Experience (N = 65) %
In care	76	84	76	63
Left care	24	16	24	37
	100	100	100	100

[a] Chi-square = 9.029 with 3 df; significant at the .03 level.

At Time 4, the picture changes again; worker experience did not play a role in the final group of discharges.

Discharge and size of case load
It was hypothesized that the lower the worker's case load, the greater the likelihood of discharge. The actual relationship at Time 1 was found to be statistically significant but it is not so simple as that suggested by the hypothesis. As Table 6.3 indicates, the number of children who were sent home was highest both for the workers with the lowest case loads *and* for those with the highest. The number of children whose disposition was undecided was highest for workers with the lowest case loads. The proportion of those awaiting long-term placement was highest for the workers with moderately low case loads. The data in the table are based on the child sample. When the same analysis was carried out with the family sample, the pattern was similar and statistically significant.

TABLE 6.3
Status of Child at Time 1 and Worker's Case Load (N = 381) [a]

Status	3–20 Cases (N = 46) %	21–30 Cases (N = 118) %	31–50 Cases (N = 89) %	51 Cases and Over (N = 128) %
At home	39	24	20	36
In long-term care	9	16	24	20
Undecided	17	14	9	5
Awaiting home	7	9	17	11
Awaiting long-term care	28	37	30	28
	100	100	100	100

[a] Chi-square = 24.963 with 12 df; significant at the .01 level.

At Time 2, the effects of case-load size involved a more complicated analysis, since this variable interacted with the type of agency involved. At this time, those children placed by the courts, where worker case loads tended to be high, had reached the 18-month limit of their original commitment, and many of them were discharged. At the same time, children placed in residential treatment centers—which are characterized by low case loads—were still likely to be continuing in treatment. To control these influences, both of these groups were eliminated from the analysis, which was then focused on the more typical long-term foster care agencies, whose range of case loads was about evenly distributed along the continuum indicated. When this was done, it was found that workers with the highest case loads, not those with the lowest, discharged children more frequently. This relationship held even when the discharged children were divided by type of agency, as in the preceding analysis.

At Time 3, the influence of the size of the case load was again bimodal, as it was at Time 1; children tended to be discharged by workers with the lowest case loads *and* by those with the highest case loads.

TABLE 6.4

Discharge at Time 2 and Case Load Size (N = 413) [a,b]

	Under 16 (N = 61)	16–23 (N = 91)	24–29 (N = 124)	30–40 (N = 86)	Over 40 (N = 51)
Status	%	%	%	%	%
In care	92	84	79	84	62
Left interim	7	8	12	7	14
Left long-term	1	8	9	9	24
	100	100	100	100	100

[a] Chi-square = 21.549; significant at .007 level with 8 df.
[b] For the analysis of discharge, the size of the Time 2 sample is larger than Time 1. Data describing 213 of the families came from workers at long-term care agencies, who were not responsible for the decision to place the child in long-term care. Therefore, their characteristics of attitudes were not relevant to the problem posed here and they were dropped from the Time 1 analysis.

TABLE 6.5

Discharge at Time 3 and Case Load Size (N = 370) [a]

	Under 15 (N = 75)	16–21 (N = 60)	22–25 (N = 78)	26–32 (N = 88)	Over 32 (N = 69)
Status	%	%	%	%	%
In care	56	83	76	89	61
Left care	44	17	24	11	39
	100	100	100	100	100

[a] Chi-square = 30.755; significant under .001 with 4 df.

At the final measure—when most of the children had been in care during all or most of the five-year span of the study—only the size of the worker's case load bore a relationship to the status of the child, but again in the same bimodal way noted earlier: those with low case loads and those with high case loads were most likely to be involved in discharges.

The children of workers with middle range case loads tended to remain in care.

TABLE 6.6

Discharge of Child at Time 4 and Caseload Size (N = 259 Children) [a]

	Under 14 (N = 47)	15–21 (N = 61)	22–25 (N = 57)	26–30 (N = 50)	Over 30 (N = 44)
Status	%	%	%	%	%
Left/about to leave	47	21	26	28	46
Remaining in care	53	79	74	72	54
	100	100	100	100	100

[a] Chi-square = 12.701; significant at .013 level with 4 df.

Discharge and Frequency of contact

It was not expected that there would be a relationship between the degree of child-centered contact and the child's discharge at Time 1, and in fact the findings showed none. Family-centered contact, on the other hand, was expected to show a relationship with discharge; and it did, as Table 6.7 indicates.

TABLE 6.7

Status of Child at Time 1 and Frequency of Family-Centered Contacts (N = 272) [a]

	Minimum Contact (N = 36)	Below Average (N = 56)	Average (N = 48)	Above Average (N = 61)	Maximum Contact (N = 71)
Status	%	%	%	%	%
Discharged	8	16	37	41	49
In care	92	84	63	59	51
	100	100	100	100	100

[a] Chi-square = 27.852; significant at .001 level, with 4 df.

It seemed safe to assume that the frequency of contact was more likely to be determined by some family member's indicated willingness to take the child home, than by a worker's intensive action with the family— although this probably has happened. However, since the proportion of children at home increased directly with the frequency of contacts, the effort itself apparently produced results even if the initiative probably came from the family.

Frequency of contact also made a contribution to discharge at Time 2, provided the child was being discharged from an agency giving long-term care. Fifty-seven percent of the children discharged during this period left from interim care agencies, the remainder left long-term care.

The analysis indicated that discharge was associated with minimum contact for those children sent home by the temporary care agencies while the reverse was true for those leaving long-term agencies. After Time 2, frequency of contact ceased to have any relationship with discharge.

TABLE 6.8

Discharge at Time 2 and Frequency of Contact (N = 492) [a]

Status	Minimal (N = 97) %	Below Average (N = 99) %	Average (N = 100) %	Above Average (N = 98) %	Maximum (N = 98) %
In care	61	86	81	88	72
Left interim	32	9	12	6	5
Left long-term	7	5	7	6	23
	100	100	100	100	100

[a] Chi-square = 66.642; significant under .001 with 8 df.

Discharge and worker stability

The child's status in placement was linked to the stability of the worker in both agencies involved in the placement situation at Time 1 (Table 6.9). When the workers from the under-care agency were represented in the analysis, nearly two-thirds of the children awaiting long-term placement had had more than one worker. When the workers from the planning agency were represented in the analysis, more than two-thirds of the children awaiting long-term care had had more than one worker. Furthermore, the number of children who returned home was markedly larger when there had been only one worker.

The reader may anticipate that the length of time in care would influence worker stability, since the longer the child was in care the greater the likelihood of staff turnover. The influence of time was checked by dividing the child sample into those in care for less than eight months and those in care for eight months or more. The analysis indicated that the relationship between the child's status and worker stability remained equally strong for both subsamples; of the children who had been await-

TABLE 6.9

Status of Child at Time 1 and Worker Stability

Status	Child Sample (N = 403) [a]		Family Sample (N = 272) [b]	
	More than one worker (N = 151) %	One worker (N = 252) %	More than one worker (N = 93) %	One worker (N = 179) %
At home	18	38	24	38
In long-term care	13	22	8	17
Undecided	13	8	5	9
Awaiting home	10	12	10	11
Awaiting long-term care	46	20	53	25
	100	100	100	100

[a] Chi-square = 40.452 with 4 df; significant at .0001 level.
[b] Chi-square = 22.521 with 4 df; significant at .0001 level.

ing long-term placement less than eight months, two-thirds had more than one worker; the same held true for children in placement more than eight months.

Worker stability continued to make a contribution to discharge at Time 2. Most of the discharges during this period occurred when the child had been in care between 13 and 17 months. Table 6.10 indicates that of the 137 study children who had been in foster care for this length of time, those who had no change in worker were more likely to be discharged than those who had one change; the latter, in turn, were more likely to be discharged than children who had had two changes of worker.

TABLE 6.10

Discharge at Time 2 and Worker Stability (N = 137) [a]

Status	Two Changes (N = 20) %	One Change (N = 46) %	No Change (N = 71) %
In care	75	54	39
Discharge	25	46	61
	100	100	100

[a] Chi-square = 8.510; significant at .015 level with 2 df.

The influence of worker stability was in the same direction at Time 3, but missed statistical significance. By Time 4, it had no impact on discharge at all.

Service Assets and Improvement in the Child

Worker Experience

At Time 1, there was no relationship between worker experience and the improvement perceived in the child. At Time 2, however—after most of the children were transferred to the care of long-term voluntary agencies—the more experienced workers were more likely to perceive improvement than the less experienced. In general, the same relationship held true for Time 3 and Time 4.

TABLE 6.11

Improvement in the Child at Time 2 and
Worker Experience (N = 389) [a]

	Minimal (N = 133) %	Moderate (N = 90) %	High (N = 166) %
Worse or unchanged	48	36	31
Some improvement	38	44	44
Marked improvement	14	20	25
	100	100	100

[a] Chi-square = 11.764; significant at .020 level with 4 df.

Case load size

At Time 1, the analysis indicated that the lower the worker's case load, the more likely she was to report improvement in the child. It was apparent, however, that this difference could be explained largely by the fact that workers with lower case loads were more knowledgeable and therefore more likely simply to be *aware* of improvement than to have *caused* it. This problem was reduced by including in the analysis of the effects of case load size only those cases where the worker's knowledge was judged by the staff to be adequate. Under this condition, improvement was still likely to be reported significantly more frequently for workers with low case loads than those with high case loads. It is worth noting, however, that the difference shown in Table 6.12 is only 10 percent, which indicates that the influence of this variable is not great, although it is apparently real and not a matter of chance fluctuations.

The size of the worker's case load is unrelated to the perception of improvement in the child at Time 2 and at Time 3, but the relationship was

TABLE 6.12

*Size of Case Load at Time 1 and Improvement
in the Child (N = 443)* [a]

	Case Load Under 30 (N = 230)	Case Load 30 and Over (N = 213)
Status	%	%
Unimproved	41	51
Improved	59	49
	100	100

[a] Chi-square = 4.336; significant at .03 level with 1 df.

seen again at Time 4, and was in the expected direction. Workers with low case loads were more likely to report improvement, workers with average or above average loads were more likely to report that the child was unchanged. Workers with high case loads were more prone to see some deterioration.

Frequency of contact

At Time 1, the relationship between frequency of contact and the perception of improvement was even stronger than that between size of case load and perception of improvement. The more frequent the contact, the greater the likelihood of perceived improvement—a relationship that held when the degree of worker's knowledge was controlled.

TABLE 6.13

Improvement in the Child at Time 4 and Case Load (N = 229) [a]

	Under 14 (N = 39)	15–21 (N = 56)	22–25 (N = 52)	26–30 (N = 44)	Over 30 (N = 38)
Status	%	%	%	%	%
Some deterioration	31	30	33	27	53
Remained the same	31	23	46	41	29
Improved	38	47	21	32	18
	100	100	100	100	100

[a] Chi-square = 18.294; significant at .020 level with 8 df.

The proportion of children for whom improvement was reported rose sharply when contact was "maximum." For the children who received attention in the "average" ranges, gains were observed—but not much more frequently than those who had minimal attention. After Time 1,

TABLE 6.14

Frequency of Child-Centered Contact and Improvement in the Child at Time 1 (N = 465) [a]

	Minimal Contact (N = 75) %	Below Average (N = 92) %	Average (N = 89) %	Above Average (N = 81) %	Maximum Contact (N = 128) %
Status					
Unimproved	57	49	49	46	33
Improved	43	51	51	54	67
	100	100	100	100	100

[a] Chi-square = 13.537; significant at .009 level with 4 df.

however, frequency of contact ceased to be a factor in the perception of improvement in the child.

Worker stability

At no time did worker turnover on the case bear a relationship to the perception of improvement in the child.

Service Assets and Improvement in the Family

When outcome defined as "perceived improvement in the family" was related to measures of "service assets," only a weak correlation could be found. This was hardly surprising, since the families involved had been carrying a heavy load of social, health, and personality problems long before the crisis that precipitated placement. The families were also much more "outside the child welfare system" (see chapter 3) than the children were; as a result they were much less likely to be influenced by that system. At Time 1, only the frequency of contact was related to the perception of improvement in the family. At Time 2, low case loads and worker stability show significant relationships. After Time 2, improvements perceived in the mother were unrelated to any of the service assets.

Frequency of contact: Time 1

As table 6.15 indicates, the more frequent the contact with the family or focused on the family, the greater the likelihood that improvement would be perceived by the worker. When the level of the worker's knowledge was controlled, the relationship remained a strong one.

It is worth noting that the families with maximum contact showed a much higher proportion of improvement than the next closest ("above average") category. As was the case with effort concentrated on the child, this is another indication that "payoff" comes largely from maximum effort and that differences are not strong below this level.

It is impossible to say whether the worker simply observed the incidence of improvement, or brought it about. Even if the difference refers only to the ability of the worker to observe change, the findings imply that frequency of contact was productive in that more strengths became visible to the worker—which may, in turn, have led to different placement decisions than those originally contemplated. In the placement situation, the worker initially sees the family in what is probably its most

TABLE 6.15

*Improvement in the Family at Time 1 and Frequency
of Family-Centered Contact (N = 380)* [a]

Status	Minimal Contact (N = 65) %	Below Average (N = 72) %	Average (N = 80) %	Above Average (N = 79) %	Maximum Contact (N = 84) %
Unimproved	60	63	58	49	30
Improved	40	37	42	51	70
	100	100	100	100	100

[a] Chi-square = 22.516; significant at .001 level with 4 df.

disturbed state; the strengths, if they are there, become apparent only with frequent contact. This is in contrast with other, more normative, social situations where strengths are initially more visible and pathology or deviant behavior becomes apparent only with frequent contact. Since the function of the workers involved at this stage of the study is primarily diagnostic, opportunity to observe whether the family is capable of improvement is actually more relevant than the workers' capacity to bring about change.

An attempt was made to assess the extent to which the worker might be contributing to improvement as well as observing it by means of a content analysis of the interview material obtained for 61 families who had been seen with maximum frequency. All workers involved could be presumed equally knowledgeable. The analysis indicated that the nature of the improvement could be divided into three categories: cases in which improvement could be attributed to the caseworker (30 percent), those in which improvement was clearly due to external sources beyond the worker's control (48 percent), and those in which the changes were a product of both worker influence and external events (22 percent).

Among the external sources contributing to improvement were, principally, release or pending release from medical or mental hospitals, being "off drugs," setting up a new family, release from prison, new employment, new living quarters, and newly developed interest in the child on the part of relatives. Improvements that could be attributed to the worker included more rational attitudes on the part of parents toward placement, greater acceptance of their children, improvement in visiting patterns, decisions to relinquish a child for adoption, and improved attitudes on the part of maternal grandparents. The most typical changes involving both worker influence and external factors were those in which mothers obtained employment after having been encouraged by the worker to seek it more actively.

Case load and worker stability: Time 2

As was indicated earlier, improvement in the family after Time 1 was assessed on the basis of the worker's opinion about the presence or absence of improvement in the mother, since the involvement of fathers or other family members was atypical. At Time 2, two of the five service assets were related to improvement in the expected direction. Workers with below average case loads were significantly more likely to perceive improvement in the mother than those with higher loads. When there was no worker turnover on a case, improvement was reported significantly more frequently than on cases where there was worker turnover (see Table 6.16).

TABLE 6.16

Improvement in the Mother at Time 2, Case Load, and Worker Stability

	Case Load (N = 184) [a]			Worker Stability (N = 186) [b]	
Status	Low (N = 84) %	Average (N = 41) %	High (N = 59) %	Stable (N = 82) %	Unstable (N = 104) %
Worse; same	38	61	56	40	56
Improved	62	39	44	60	44
	100	100	100	100	100

[a] Chi-square = 7.485; significant at .024 level with 2 df.
[b] Chi-square = 4.423; significant at .036 level with 1 df.

Summary

An analysis of the impact of service assets on the discharge of children from foster care and perception of improvement in the child and in the family revealed the following patterns:

1. If the worker on the case remained on it, this contributed to the discharge rate within the first two years of placement, but not later.
2. The more frequent the contact of the worker with the child and his family, the greater the likelihood of discharge within the first year of placement. In the second year, there was a positive relationship only when the child was discharged from a long-term agency. From the second year on, there was no relationship.
3. Workers with either low or high case loads tended to discharge children more frequently than those with average loads, except at Time 2, when only the high case load was related to discharge.
4. The more experienced the worker at the child-caring agency during the first year of placement, the more likely the child was to be discharged. This relationship did not hold for Times 2 and 4, but did hold for Time 3.
5. At Time 1, the only service asset significantly related to perception of improvement in the child was the frequency of contact. After that, frequency ceased to be important in relation to this outcome.
6. After the first year in placement, worker experience was significantly related to the perception of improvement in the child at each point in time.
7. Workers with relatively low case loads perceived improvement in the child only at the time of the final measures.
8. Worker stability showed no relationship with improvement in the child at any point in time.
9. When related to improvement in the mother, positive relationships were found between frequency of contact at Time 1 and between low case loads and no worker turnover at Time 2. After that, improvement reported by the workers was not linked with any of the measures of agency investment examined here.

Discussion

Before comment on the general implications of the findings, several specific findings warrant some discussion. It seems paradoxical that, in the critical first year, the experience of the worker carrying responsibility for the placement decision had little influence on the child's status while the experience of the worker at the child caring agency was influential. However, it was evident from our interview data that under-care workers attached a variety of interpretations to their function. Some took the division of responsibility literally and played the prescribed secondary role, confining themselves to the liaison work or concentrating their efforts entirely on the child. Others were much more active in involving themselves with the family and in cooperating actively with the planning worker. Although such dual divisions of responsibility are usually perceived as a burden for the worker and a source of confusion for the client, the data indicate that the presence of the second worker can benefit the client, if the worker has activist inclinations and is willing to take on the additional burden of potential conflict with a cooperating agency. It is also evident from the data that it is largely the experienced workers who act on such inclinations.

The other seeming paradox is the repeated finding that children are more likely to be discharged by workers with low case loads *and* by workers with high case loads, instead of the expected association between higher case load and lower likelihood of discharge. Seemingly even more paradoxical was the finding that, at Time 1, workers with the lowest case loads were the ones least likely to discharge their clients from interim care.

One may speculate that workers with the highest case loads feel the pressure to make a decision more strongly than others. Hence they are more likely to force a decision than to allow themselves to defer it, even when this might be appropriate. Conversely, workers with lower case loads may feel that they can take a longer time to insure a sounder decision and defer sending a child home while they work with the mother. At any rate, high case loads apparently do not always lead to slow decision-making, as is commonly supposed. The size of the case load may mean a different approach to its management, not necessarily diminished efficiency.

The first-year findings imply that frequency of contact with clients is the most important of the several factors linked to favorable outcome. Worker stability and lower case loads are related to frequency of contact and probably provide the conditions that permit such frequency, but are not identical with it. Frequency of effort within a short period of time may be more productive than a more extended effort over a longer period. The client may benefit as much, if not more, from a reorganization of the worker's time—which, for instance, might reduce the amount of administrative detail or traveling time—as he would from a reduced case load; although he also benefits from this factor, as the data indicate.

The full evidence of the five-year pattern described indicates that those features which social work practice has traditionally considered "good" are in fact "good"—but largely in the early stages of the foster care process. The contradiction of the system as it is presently structured in New York City lies in the fact that the quality of the service given improves after the first year but the opportunity to exploit higher quality is optimal in the first year. It stands to reason that if service assets contribute to discharge in the first year, a considerably higher rate of movement out of the system could be obtained if the present situation were reversed and the "service assets" enhanced in the first year, rather than later. The same implications can be drawn in relation to the findings with respect to improvement in the mother. If improvement is perceived more frequently by workers in relatively frequent contact, with low case loads, and who do not leave within the first two years of placement, it follows that much knowledge of the capacity of the mother to change is lost by virtue of the absence of such conditions in the first year of placement—and, along with it, the opportunity for an earlier discharge.

chapter seven

WORKERS' ATTITUDES AND OTHER INFLUENCES ON OUTCOME

Foster Care

IN A FIELD which depends heavily on individual judgments and whose principal techniques are still based on one-to-one relationships, the attitudes of the workers toward the children and the mothers they serve are bound to play a significant role in relation to discharge. As was noted in chapter 1, the inclusion of the analysis of such "soft" variables always presents the researcher with more difficult measurement problems and more unreliable results than do the more objective and more readily quantifiable variables described in the previous chapter as "service assets." Nevertheless, it was untenable to overlook the subjective reactions or assessments of workers, and those indices of worker attitudes which could be derived from the data were given considerable attention in the analysis.

In general, the analysis indicated that the workers' attitudes toward the child bore little relation to discharge. Attitudes toward the mother, in contrast, were significant at each time cycle. This is not surprising, since the workers' evaluation of the mother's capacities is obviously a basic consideration in discharge. What is more meaningful is that this evaluation is equal in its influence on discharge to the worker's experience, stability, the size of her caseload, and the frequency of contact in the early phases of placement; it outweighs in importance client and agency characteristics that affect discharge in later phases of placement. Also significant is that the worker's attitude not only predicts discharge at the same time cycle but at the succeeding one as well.

When perceived improvements in the mother or the child were treated as outcomes, workers' attitudes were, as expected, closely related to their judgments of improvement. When judgments of improvement in the child were made at a later time cycle, independently of the previous workers' position, the findings indicated that a worker's evaluation of the child at one time cycle did not predict improvement at a later time cycle. The worker's evaluation of the mother, on the other hand, did predict a judgment of improvement at the succeeding time cycle. In other words, the workers' evaluations of the capacities of the mothers they worked with and their attitudes toward them were apparently more stable than their evaluations of the children.

Worker characteristics and attitudes are obviously not the only variables related to discharge. Client characteristics such as age, sex, race, ethnicity, marital status of the mother, legitimacy of the child, intelligence test scores, and socioeconomic status were examined in relation to both forms of outcome, along with such aspects of agency structure as public or voluntary auspices, sectarian affiliation, and type, size, and complexity of service. The importance of these characteristics varied in each time cycle but, in general, they did not have so much influence as the worker characteristics noted.

Worker's Evaluation
of the Mother and Discharge

At each time cycle, an index was developed which reflected the worker's assessment of the mother. These indices included such items as the worker's opinion of the mother's capacity to function as a mother, the degree of emotional disturbance seen, her opinion about the outlook for working with the mother, her prediction as to the likelihood that the mother would lose contact with the agency, the extent to which the mother made use of her visiting privileges, the extent to which the mother was disturbed by separation from her child, the worker's perception of the mother's attitude toward her and the agency, and the interviewer's assessment of the worker's interest in the mother. The content of the index used at each time cycle was not identical, since some items that correlated highly with others at one cycle did not necessarily do so at others.

Nevertheless, it was felt that each index was a fair approximation of the worker's attitude and that all four were comparable in intent. Thus, in general, a mother who was perceived by the worker as generally adequate, not too severely disturbed—one who could be "worked with," who was unlikely to drift away from agency contact while the child continued in care, who visited as much as possible, who resented or felt guilty about continued separation from her child, who had a positive attitude toward the worker and the agency, and in whose case the interviewer also judged the worker's attitude to be one of interest and support—received a high score on this index; those with the reverse tendencies were the low scorers.

As Table 7.1 indicates, the mothers who were evaluated in the most negative terms at Time 1 had children who were nearly always continu-

TABLE 7.1

Worker's Evaluation of Mother and Discharge at Time 1 (N = 245) [a]

	Negative (N = 48)	Somewhat Negative (N = 41)	Mixed (N = 48)	Somewhat Positive (N = 54)	Positive (N = 54)
Status	%	%	%	%	%
Discharged	10	24	31	35	52
In Care	90	76	69	65	48
	100	100	100	100	100

[a] Chi-square = 21.581; significant under .001 with 4 df.

ing in care. Those who impressed the worker most favorably were the most likely to have had children who were discharged. Children of those with "in-between" ratings were more likely than not to continue in care.

The regression analysis indicated that the worker's evaluation of the mother was equal in influence to that of frequency of contact, as noted in the previous chapter. These two variables were, as one would expect, related to one another: the mothers who were seen more frequently also tended to be more favorably evaluated. Yet the favorable evaluation retained its influence on discharge even when the degree of contact was controlled.

At Time 2, the worker's attitude continued to be influential in relation to discharge but not so strongly as at Time 1. This time the differences were between the mothers in the two lowest categories on the scale— most of whose children remained in care—and those mothers with a "mixed" rating or better. They were somewhat more likely to have discharged children, even though the majority also continued in care.

The worker's evaluation of the mother was related to one of the two service assets which were influential at this time; if the worker did not change during the time period covered, the mother was more likely to be seen in favorable terms. Nevertheless, the regression analysis indicated again that the worker's evaluation contributed to discharge, even when the turnover variable was controlled.

At the next time cycle, when the influence of the service assets began to diminish, the worker's attitude toward the mother continued to be an important factor in discharge. Like the Time 2 pattern, the difference was largely between those mothers at the lowest end of the scale and all the

TABLE 7.2

Worker's Evaluation of the Mother and Discharge at Time 2 (N = 369) [a]

Status	Negative (N = 40) %	Somewhat Negative (N = 107) %	Mixed (N = 75) %	Somewhat Positive (N = 73) %	Positive (N = 74) %
Discharged	10	14	25	25	31
In Care	90	86	75	75	69
	100	100	100	100	100

[a] Chi-square = 11.826; significant at .019 with 4 df.

others. A mother whose worker made a "mixed" assessment of her abilities was just as likely to have her child discharged as one whose worker saw her in a much more positive light.

The Time 3 regression analysis indicated, however, that another variable was even more influential in relation to discharge than the worker's evaluation of the mother. This was the extent to which the mother was passive about the child's placement or actively interested in having him discharged. At this time, three and a half years after placement, 28 percent of the mothers still known to the agency were characterized by their workers as having failed to verbalize feelings about continuation of placement, as wanting no involvement, or as feeling that they had no choice in the matter; 16 percent were described as accepting placement as a positive solution to their problems, and preferring it to the alternative of taking their children home; 38 percent had, according to their workers,

TABLE 7.3

*Worker's Evaluation of the Mother and Discharge
at Time 3 (N = 294)* [a]

Status	Negative (N = 27) %	Somewhat Negative (N = 92) %	Mixed (N = 57) %	Somewhat Positive (N = 59) %	Positive (N = 59) %
Discharged	7	13	37	44	37
In Care	93	87	63	56	63
	100	100	100	100	100

[a] Chi-square = 28.030; significant at .001 with 4 df.

mixed feelings—i.e., missing the child but doing little to change the situation. Only 18 percent were characterized as openly rejecting the continuation of placement and working toward taking the child home, but this group accounts for more than 40 percent of the discharges that took place at this time. That the mother's ability to act should be an important influence in discharge again is not surprising. The noteworthy aspect of this relationship is that her determination outweighs in influence many other variables that also showed significant relationships with discharge.[1]

At Time 4, the worker's evaluation of the mother was again the most influential variable, accounting for more of the variance on discharge than any other. The only other variable that continued to be influential when others were controlled was the worker's case load, but the influence

TABLE 7.4

*Mothers' Feelings about Separation and Discharge
at Time 3 (N = 203)* [a]

Status	Passive Acceptance (N = 57) %	Positive Acceptance (N = 32) %	Mixed (N = 78) %	Active Rejection (N = 36) %
Discharged	14	28	24	75
In Care	86	72	76	25
	100	100	100	100

[a] Chi-square = 41.959; significant under .001 with 3 df.

1. These included such worker characteristics as experience, case load, degree of pressure, sex, age, knowledge of the case, attitude toward the child, such client characteristics as reason for placement, race, age, socioeconomic and marital status of the mother, and such agency characteristics as the size and sectarian affiliation of the agency.

of this variable was unrelated to that of the worker's attitude. As at Time 1, only the children of mothers whose evaluation by the workers was the most positive tended to be discharged.

Children of mothers rated "mixed" by the workers were just as likely to continue in care as those of mothers with negative ratings.

The general impression, then, is that in the first year of placement and in the fifth year, the mother's impact on the worker needed to be strongly positive to effect a discharge. In the intervening years, workers were apparently more willing to give the benefit of the doubt or were more responsive to pressure from the mother, or else the influence of the court was felt in those cases under their jurisdiction.

These findings raise the question, as many research findings do, of circularity. The data used in the indices and information about the cir-

TABLE 7.5

Worker's Evaluation of Mother and Discharge
at Time 4 (N = 145) [a]

Status	Negative (N = 48) %	Mixed (N = 45) %	Positive (N = 52) %
Discharged	25	27	64
In Care	75	73	26
	100	100	100

[a] Chi-square = 19.849; significant at .001 with 2 df.

cumstances under which the decision to discharge was made were obtained from the same respondent at the same time. It is conceivable that a worker reporting a discharge from care would paint a more favorable picture of a mother who has been allowed to take her child home—and so justify the discharge—than the one she might have painted were the child continuing in care.

To test this possibility, the worker's attitude toward the mother was related to the child's status at the following time cycle, when the date of discharge was considerably later than the date of the evaluation and, in most instances, was reported by another worker. The findings indicated that mothers who were favorably evaluated at Time 1 were somewhat more likely to have their children discharged by Time 2, but this trend just missed statistical significance. A positive evaluation of the mother at Time 2, however, clearly predicted discharge at Time 3. Forty-three percent of the mothers whose workers evaluated them positively had children who had been discharged, in contrast to 16 percent of those whose evaluation was negative (significant at .002). The same pattern was seen at Time 4: 58 percent of the mothers with the most positive Time 3 evaluations had children who were discharged as against 26 percent of those who had been negatively evaluated (significant at .01).

Other Factors Influencing Discharge

The analysis indicated that some client and some agency characteristics were influential in the earlier phases of placement. At Time 1, children placed because of the mother's illness were much more likely to be discharged than children placed for other reasons. This variable was unrelated to any of the other variables which were seen as significant at this time.

TABLE 7.6

Reason for Placement and Discharge at Time 1 (N = 403) [a]

Status	Physical Illness of Mother (N = 63) %	All Others (N = 340) %
Discharged	48	27
In Care	52	73
	100	100

[a] Chi-square = 9.361; significant at .003 with 1 df.

At Time 2, another reason for placement became an important factor in discharge. Children placed because of neglect were more likely to be discharged than children placed for other reasons.

This may seem surprising but, as was noted in chapter 1, children placed through the courts were remanded for a period of 18 months. At

TABLE 7.7

Reason for Placement and Discharge at Time 2 (N = 471) [a]

Status	Neglect (N = 107) %	All Others (N = 364) %
Discharged	33	19
In Care	67	81
	100	100

[a] Chi-square = 9.092; significant at .003 with 1 df.

the end of this time, the case would be reviewed and the child would
often be sent home to his parents—apparently for lack of evidence sufficiently strong to warrant continuation in placement. As Table 7.2 indicates, the mothers about whom workers had "mixed" feelings were as
likely as those whose assessment was more positive to have their children
discharged at this time. Again, such a pattern suggests that in many of
these decisions either the family received the benefit of the doubt or a
less-than-ideal home was judged to be the lesser of the evils. Furthermore, some informants indicated that many of the children in the "neglect" category were not literally neglected but presented behavior problems and were in need of closer supervision than their families were able
to give them. Placement through a neglect petition, rather than through

TABLE 7.8

Agency Characteristics and Discharge at Time 2

	Type of Placement (N = 459) [a]		Religious Affiliation (N = 493) [b]	
	Institutional placements (N = 241)	Foster home placements (N = 218)	Catholic Agencies (N = 248)	Non-Catholic Agencies (N = 245)
Status	%	%	%	%
Discharged	24	8	19	26
In Care	76	92	81	74
	100	100	100	100

[a] Chi-square = 20.706; significant under .001 with 1 df.
[b] Chi-square = 4.079; significant at .04 with 1 df.

the more appropriate designation of "persons-in-need-of-supervision"
(PINS) simply afforded the probation officers a wider choice of placement
possibilities than they would have had for PINS cases, for whom the principal resources were institutions for juvenile delinquents.

Two agency characteristics also influenced discharge at Time 2. Children were more likely to leave institutional care than foster home care
and they were more likely to leave non-Catholic than Catholic agencies.

Again, the first variable was related to influential variables noted earlier. Mothers of children in institutions tended to be evaluated more
highly than those whose children were placed in foster homes. Despite
this relationship, the analysis indicated that placement in an institution
was in itself a factor associated with discharge, even when the worker's at-

titude toward the mother was held constant. Why Catholic agencies were apparently more conservative than others at this time is harder to explain. The difference, however, is only 7 percent, and although it is unlikely to be a matter of chance, the trend is not so strong as that of the other differences noted. It is worth noting, however, that Maas, in following-up the national sample described in *Children in Need of Parents*, also found an association between long-term care and the Catholic religion; he suggested that "Catholic agencies operate on somewhat different principles of child care than do other agencies." [2]

At Time 3, two client variables were influential, even when the mother's feelings about separation were controlled. One of these variables was again the reason for placement. If the child was placed initially because of his own emotional disturbance, he was far more likely to have

TABLE 7.9

Ethnicity and Discharge at Time 3 (N = 389) [a]

Status	White (N = 103) %	Black; Puerto Rican (N = 286) %
Discharged	48	22
In Care	52	78
	100	100

[a] Chi-square = 23.646; significant under .001, with 1 df.

been discharged at Time 3 than any of the children placed for other reasons. Sixty-seven percent of the children placed for emotional disturbance left care, in contrast to 25 percent of the rest of the sample. The ethnicity of the child was also an important factor in discharge at this time. As Table 7.9 indicates, white children were more than twice as likely to leave care than black or Puerto Rican children.

The white discharge rate was higher than that of the black and Puerto Rican children at each of the four time cycles, but the influence of this variable usually disappears when it is introduced into the analysis together with other variables to which ethnicity is related. At Time 3, however, it retained its influence even when related variables were controlled. In other words, children placed because of emotional disturbance, who were preponderantly white, tended to be discharged at this time, but the fact of being white also contributed significantly to the discharge rate.

2. Henry S. Maas, "Children in Long-Term Foster Care," *Child Welfare* 48, no. 6 (June 1969): 323.

By Time 4, no client or agency variable was influential in relation to discharge.

Influences on Improvement in the Family

Not surprisingly, the worker's attitude toward the mother predicted her judgment of improvement as did her optimism about the potential for discharge. At Time 1, improvement was seen in 40 percent of the families in the total sample but was reported for 66 percent of those cases where there was a positive evaluation of the mother. At Time 2, the picture was similar: improvement for the family sample as a whole was seen in 37 percent of the cases still in care but the rate was 65 percent for those where there was a positive evaluation of the mother.

TABLE 7.10

Worker Optimism and Improvement in the Family at Time 2 and Time 3

	Time 2 (N = 194) [a]			Time 3 (N = 177) [b]		
	Pessimistic (N = 44)	50–50 (N = 49)	Optimistic (N = 101)	Pessimistic (N = 84)	50–50 (N = 36)	Optimistic (N = 57)
Status	%	%	%	%	%	%
Unimproved	89	57	55	45	28	17
Improved	11	43	45	55	72	83
	100	100	100	100	100	100

[a] Chi-square = 15.657; significant under .001 with 2 df.
[b] Chi-square = 12.331; significant under .01 with 2 df.

At Time 3, the index measure used showed no relation to reports of improvement but the worker's statement about the mother's competence did. Thirty-four percent of the mothers known to the agency three years after placement were considered adequate and improvement was reported for 63 percent. At Time 4, 37 percent of the mothers were evaluated in positive terms by their workers and improvement was seen for 56 percent of these. Except for Time 3, the worker's evaluation of the mother accounted for more of the variance in family improvement than any other variable.

At Times 2 and 3, other attitudes were also significantly related to reports of improvement. One index called "optimism-pessimism" was composed of the predictions made by each worker at each time cycle as to whether the child was likely to return home, how long he would remain in care, whether he had any chance of being adopted, and whether his parents were likely to be agency "drop-outs." At both points in time, the more optimistic the worker, the more likely she was to see improvement.

These findings raise the question of circularity even more insistently than those related to discharge, since not only are these data obtained from the same respondent in the course of a single interview but all are attitudinal measures as well. Did the worker obtain the information on which she based her evaluation of the mother first and perceive improvement later, or did she see some improvement which then caused her to see the mother in more positive terms?

TABLE 7.11

Worker's Evaluation of Mother at Time 2 and Improvement at Time 3
(N = 288) [a]

	Negative (N = 37)	Somewhat Negative (N = 89)	Mixed (N = 57)	Somewhat Positive (N = 54)	Positive (N = 51)
Status	%	%	%	%	%
Deteriorated	16	30	14	6	10
Unimproved	16	16	21	22	12
Slight Improvement	36	20	30	24	19
Improved	16	15	21	18	20
Marked Improvement	16	19	14	30	39
	100	100	100	100	100

[a] Chi-square = 32.170; significant at .01 with 16 df.

To deal with this problem, the procedure noted earlier in relation to the question of discharge was followed again. The worker's evaluation of the mother was cross-tabulated against the judgment of improvement obtained at the succeeding time cycle, where both assessments could be assumed to be independent of one another.

When the Time 1 evaluation of the mother was compared to the Time 2 judgment of improvement, no relationship was found. This may be related to the fact that the Time 1 judgment was made under the weakest conditions, based as it was on a minimum of knowledge by the least trained workers with the least contact and so was more likely to be haphazard than those made later. From Time 2 on, as Tables 7.11 and 7.12 indicate, a positive assessment on the part of the worker predicts a judgment of improvement at the later cycle, again supporting the inference made earlier that workers' attitudes toward mothers are relatively stable, despite time and turnover.

TABLE 7.12

Worker's Evaluation of Mother at Time 3 and Improvement at Time 4
(N = 135) [a]

	Negative (N = 16)	Somewhat Negative (N = 40)	Mixed (N = 24)	Somewhat Positive (N = 21)	Positive (N = 34)
Status	%	%	%	%	%
Unimproved	81	75	71	71	44
Improved	19	25	29	29	56
	100	100	100	100	100

[a] Chi-square = 10.962; significant at .028 with 4 df.

As with discharge, workers' attitudes toward the mother are not the only factors related to their perception of improvement. Of the disturbances described by them at Time 1, workers were particularly prone to see improvement in two groups of mothers: those for whom there was evidence of mental illness and those considered emotionally "normal"— i.e., whose placement problem was precipitated by a medical illness or an unwanted pregnancy.

The first relationship is not surprising; many of the early placements for "mental illness" were characterized as stress reactions from which the

TABLE 7.13

Mother's Emotional State and Improvement Perceived at Time 1

	Mental Illness (N = 104) [a]	All Others (N = 354) [a]	"Normal" (N = 68) [b]	All Others (N = 390) [b]
Status	%	%	%	%
Unimproved	44	67	43	65
Improved	56	33	57	35
	100	100	100	100

[a] Chi-square = 16.623; significant at .001 with 1 df.
[b] Chi-square = 11.461; significant under .001 with 1 df.

mother was able to recover. The "normal" group included mothers whose medical problems were amenable to treatment and mothers with unwanted pregnancies who could resolve their dilemma with a decision to place the baby for adoption or persuade their families to help them keep the child; therefore they did not usually need prolonged care.

Of the agency variables examined, one showed a significant relationship with improvement or the lack of it. Mothers whose children were placed in long-term institutional care were significantly less likely to be perceived as having improved than mothers whose children were cared for elsewhere. Contrary to what one might assume at first glance, the age of the mothers of institutionalized children—which is relatively older—shows no significant relationship with improvement. It seems more likely that changes in the mother may have been less visible in the long-term institutional settings than they were in temporary settings or in foster homes. Since this relationship disappears after Time 1, it may be that workers were less motivated to deal with parents when the children had just begun to settle into long-term institutional care or it may simply have taken them longer to know the family of the child who is a relatively recent arrival.

TABLE 7.14

Type of Care and Improvement in the Family at Time 1 (N = 458) [a]

	Long-Term Institutions (N = 123)	All Others (N = 335)
Status	%	%
Unimproved	71	59
Improved	29	41
	100	100

[a] Chi-square = 5.188; significant at .023 with 1 df.

At Time 4, the only variable which predicted improvement in the mother during the same period, apart from the worker's attitude, was her visiting pattern. While it was usually part of the worker's evaluation, visiting accounted for a significant degree of variance in improvement, independently of the worker's attitude.

TABLE 7.15

Mother's Visiting Pattern and Worker's Perception of Improvement at Time 4 (N = 117) [a]

	Minimal Visiting (N = 49)	Some Visiting (N = 25)	Maximum Visiting (N = 43)
Status	%	%	%
Unimproved	80	68	54
Improved	20	32	46
	100	100	100

[a] Chi-square = 7.119; significant at .029 with 2 df.

In dealing with the problem of circularity, it was found that two non-attitudinal variables also predicted movement in the family at later stages in placement. In those cases where the father was present, agency involvement with him at Time 2 predicted improvement in the family at Time 3. It is noteworthy that the response was bimodal. Improvement was seen most often both when the father was totally absent and when he was a frequent visitor. Minimal contact predicts the least improvement.

TABLE 7.16

Agency Contact with Fathers at Time 2 and Improvement in the Family at Time 3 (N = 138) [a]

	No Contact (N = 34)	Minimal Contact (N = 47)	Frequent Contact (N = 57)
Status	%	%	%
Unimproved	18	51	37
Slight Improvement	41	15	26
Improved	41	34	37
	100	100	100

[a] Chi-square = 11.459; significant at .05 with 4 df.

Another variable related to improvement in the family at Time 3 was its dependency on public assistance, but the relationship here is the reverse of what some might expect. The family receiving assistance at Time 2 was significantly more likely to be perceived as improved by Time 3 than the non–public assistance family.

When one considers that most of the families involved in foster care

TABLE 7.17

Public Assistance at Time 2 and Improvement in the Family at Time 3 (N = 286) [a]

	Public Assistance (N = 102)	Non–Public Assistance (N = 184)
Status	%	%
Deteriorated	8	22
Unimproved	16	18
Slight Improvement	29	22
Improved	19	17
Marked Improvement	28	21
	100	100

[a] Chi-square = 11.194; significant at .025 with 4 df.

are single-parent families, it may be that public assistance, usually thought of as dysfunctional, here serves the more positive purpose of freeing the mother from the necessity of working, thus permitting her to recuperate from a mental or a physical illness at home. Consequently the likelihood will increase that she will be able to devote more positive attention to her children, with the resultant improvement in the general state of the family.

Two variables at Time 3 predicted improvement at Time 4: the worker's optimism about discharge and changes in the economic situation. At

TABLE 7.18

Worker Optimism at Time 3 and Improvement in the Family at Time 4
(N = 105)

	Pessimistic (N = 50)	50–50 (N = 19)	Optimistic (N = 36)
Status	%	%	%
Unimproved	72	74	41
Improved	28	26	59
	100	100	100

Chi-square = 9.530; significant at .01 with 2 df.

Time 3, workers were asked if changes had taken place in the family situation in the years since the last measure. The changes most commonly described related to employment. These were categorized as negative (loss of job), and positive (new employment, entry into training programs, etc.). Several other forms of change, such as alterations in family structure, were also described; but only the economic changes predicted workers' perceptions of improvement or the lack of it at Time 4.

TABLE 7.19

Changes in the Economic Situation of the Family at Time 3 and
Improvement at Time 4 (N = 134) [a]

	No Change (N = 92)	Negative Change (N = 22)	Positive Change (N = 20)
Status	%	%	%
Unimproved	66	86	45
Improved	34	14	55
	100	100	100

[a] Chi-square = 8.038; significant at .019 with 2 df.

Worker Attitudes and Other Factors
Related to the Perception of
Improvement in Children

Workers perceived improvement in children not only when they had relatively frequent contact with them, as was indicated in chapter 6, but
they were also more likely to see improvement when their initial evaluation of the child's capacities—his health, emotional state, intelligence,
developmental level, etc.—was low. Half the children seen as unchanged
during the period covered by the Time 1 interview had maintained themselves during this initial period of placement. Marked improvement was
more apt to be noted among children whose capacities were initially assessed as low. This is not surprising when one considers that many children were placed after long periods of deprivation, changes in parent figures, and other traumas. Dramatic reactions to the relative stability of a
good foster home or a stable institutional setting were fairly frequently
noted by the workers.

TABLE 7.20

Worker Evaluation of the Child at Time 1 and the Perception of Improvement
at Time 1 (N = 607) [a]

	Poor Condition (N = 114) %	Below Average (N = 122) %	Average (N = 127) %	Above Average (N = 118) %	Good Condition (N = 126) %
Status					
Same	33	43	46	57	63
Some Improvement	49	48	46	36	31
Marked Improvement	18	9	8	7	6
	100	100	100	100	100

[a] Chi-square = 35.470; significant under .001 with 8 df.

Independently of this relationship, the analysis indicated that children
whom workers found "appealing" were also likely to be seen as improved.

The workers' perception of improvement at Time 2 presented a somewhat more complicated picture, since a number of variables were associated with it that were not necessarily related to one another. Again,
the worker's evaluation of the child was related to her perception of im-

TABLE 7.21

Appeal of the Child and Improvement at Time 1 (N = 607) [a]

	Unappealing (N = 111)	Somewhat Unappealing (N = 130)	Average (N = 120)	Somewhat Appealing (N = 98)	Very Appealing (N = 148)
Status	%	%	%	%	%
Remained Same	62	42	39	46	54
Some Improvement	33	48	52	46	33
Marked Improvement	5	10	9	8	13
	100	100	100	100	100

[a] Chi-square = 23.476; significant at .003 with 8 df.

provement, but in contrast to the situation at Time 1, it was the children who were seen in very negative terms—low intelligence, disturbed behavior, poor adjustment to placement—and who were also seen as either deteriorated or unchanged. Children evaluated in more positive terms were more likely to be seen as improved.

Another factor involved in the perception of improvement was the nature of the child's disturbance. Those children whose problems were described as anxieties or fears specifically related to the placement situation were more likely than any other group to be reported as improved.

TABLE 7.22

Evaluation of the Child and Improvement at Time 2 (N = 491) [a]

	Poor Condition (N = 96)	Below Average (N = 101)	Average (N = 93)	Above Average (N = 91)	Good Condition (N = 110)
Status	%	%	%	%	%
Deteriorated; unimproved	48	18	20	11	4
Slight Improvement	18	17	24	22	16
Some Improvement	9	24	20	23	23
Improvement	9	19	16	21	33
Marked Improvement	16	22	20	23	24
	100	100	100	100	100

[a] Chi-square = 81.777; significant under .001 with 16 df.

TABLE 7.23

Placement-Centered Anxiety and Improvement at Time 2 (N = 255) [a]

Status	Anxiety (N = 40) %	All Other Problems (N = 215) %
Deteriorated	13	27
Same; slight	25	34
Improved	35	17
Marked Improvement	27	22
	100	100

[a] Chi-square = 9.972; significant at the .02 level with 2 df.

Two organizational variables also were related to improvement at Time 2. Children in the care of public agencies were much more likely to be seen as deteriorating than those in the care of voluntary agencies. Children in foster homes were more likely to be seen as improving than those in institutions.

TABLE 7.24

Agency Auspices, Type of Care, and the Perception of Improvement in the Child at Time 2

Status	(N = 494)		(N = 459)	
	Public (N = 87) [a] %	Voluntary (N = 407) [a] %	Institutions (N = 241) [b] %	Foster Homes (N = 218) [b] %
Deteriorated	44	15	24	12
Same	26	17	21	15
Slight Improvement	15	21	19	23
Improved	9	23	18	24
Marked Improvement	6	24	18	26
	100	100	100	100

[a] Chi-square = 53.516; significant under .001 with 4 df.
[b] Chi-square = 17.373; significant at .002 with 4 df.

That the children still in public agency care at Time 2 fell so heavily in the "deteriorated" category is not surprising, since these were the retarded and the severely disturbed who presented particularly difficult placement problems and remained longest in the city-run shelters. Why foster home children should be seen as improved more readily than institutional children is not so apparent. The analysis indicated that this was not a function of the age difference between the two groups. It seems more likely that the worker's more individualized contacts with foster mothers and the latter's ability to observe the child together with personal investment, produced more reports of improvement than the more diluted reports workers may have had from institutional counselors who relate to larger groups of children, with possibly less individualization.

At Time 3, the worker's negative evaluation of a child was associated with a judgment that his condition had deteriorated during the time covered. A stronger predictor of improvement, however, was the child's behavior at school. Children reported to be showing serious behavior problems were also likely to be seen as getting worse generally.

TABLE 7.25

School Behavior and Improvement at Time 3 (N = 267) [a]

Status	Serious Problems (N = 23) %	Mild Problems (N = 58) %	None (N = 186) %
Deteriorated	52	28	13
Same; slight Improvement	31	40	41
Improved	4	15	22
Marked Improvement	13	17	24
	100	100	100

[a] Chi-square = 26.101; significant at .001 with 6 df.

Since the judgment of improvement in the child presented the same problems of circularity noted earlier in relation to attitudes for the mother, a series of variables describing the child at an earlier cycle was run against improvement perceived in the succeeding cycle. This analysis produced almost no significant relationships. In other words, workers' evaluations or attitudes toward the child at one point did not in turn predict the same evaluations or attitudes at later stages nor did they predict improvement at later stages. Again it would seem that the workers' perceptions of children were much less stable than their perceptions of mothers. One exception, however, to the rule of unrelatedness between assessments at different time cycles was that the more positive the evaluation of the mother at Time 2 the greater the likelihood of marked improvement *in the child* at Time 3.

At Time 4, the worker's evaluation of the child again predicted her perception of improvement, but the analysis indicated that other variables were more powerful predictors. The child's school behavior was again related to the perception of improvement, as it was at Time 3.

The child's reaction to placement was also, not surprisingly, a predic-

TABLE 7.26

Evaluation of the Mother at Time 2 and Improvement in the Child at Time 3 (N = 382) [a]

	Negative (N = 170)	Mixed (N = 73)	Positive (N = 139)
Status	%	%	%
Deteriorated	21	22	16
Unimproved	26	18	11
Slight Improvement	23	19	21
Some Improvement	15	22	22
Marked Improvement	15	19	30
	100	100	100

[a] Chi-square = 21.479; significant under .01 with 8 df.

tor of improvement. The more positive the child's attitude toward the fact that he was in foster care, the more likely the worker was to perceive improvement.

Another relationship, again not a surprise, was that the better the qual-

TABLE 7.27

School Behavior and Improvement in the Child at Time 4 (N = 225) [a]

	School Difficulties (N = 54)	No School Difficulties (N = 171)
Status	%	%
Unimproved	56	28
Some Improvement	22	37
Marked Improvement	22	35
	100	100

[a] Chi-square = 13.697; significant under .01 with 2 df.

ity of the casework relationship, as described by the worker, the more likely the worker was to perceive improvement. Of the 226 children still in care at Time 4 and involved in a casework relationship, 39 percent of these relationships were described as superficial. For 43 percent, a relationship was beginning to be established, and for 18 percent the rela-

TABLE 7.28

Child's Reaction to Placement and Improvement at Time 4 (N = 242) [a]

	Negative; Mixed (N = 72)	Positive (N = 131)	Very Positive (N = 39)
Status	%	%	%
Unimproved	48	27	31
Some Improvement	20	44	28
Marked Improvement	32	29	41
	100	100	100

[a] Chi-square = 16.033; significant at .01 with 4 df.

tionship was described as "intensive." Reports of marked improvement were most likely to come from this last group.

These variables again raise the chronic question of circularity. Naturally, the child who does well in school, is glad to be in a foster home,

TABLE 7.29

Quality of Casework and Improvement in the Child at Time 4 [a] *(N = 226)*

	Superficial (N = 89)	Some Relationship (N = 96)	Intensive (N = 41)
Status	%	%	%
Unimproved	44	31	22
Improved	34	38	32
Marked Improvement	22	31	46¿
	100	100	100

[a] Chi-square = 10.012; significant at .041 with 4 df.

and is being seen frequently by his case worker is the one most likely to be seen as improving. No variable based on more objective information was found to be clearly associated with this perception of improvement, which again suggests that such judgments are somewhat haphazard.

Workers' Predictions

In earlier references to the optimism-pessimism index, workers were asked to predict—at each cycle of data collection—what chance they thought the child had of returning home. The changes in this pattern of prediction over time were described in chapter 3. The five-year time span of the study also permitted us to examine the accuracy of the workers' predictions and whether the degree of accuracy changed with time. The findings indicated that while most of the workers were generally correct, some differences in the direction of their errors are meaningful. Table 7.30 illustrates the relationship between the Time 1 worker's predictions that the child will return home and his status at the end of the study.

TABLE 7.30

Time 1 Worker's Prediction and Child's Status Five Years after Placement [a]
(N = 471) [b]

	No Chance (N = 60)	Slight Chance (N = 97)	Some Chance (N = 57)	Fair Chance (N = 109)	Good Chance (N = 61)	Strong Chance (N = 87)
Status	%	%	%	%	%	%
In Care	65	60	51	51	36	21
Discharged	35	40	49	49	64	79
	100	100	100	100	100	100

[a] Children already discharged at Time 1 were not included.
[b] Chi-square = 42.156; significant under .001 with 5 df.

The workers who chose the middle response of "some chance" or "50–50" were in effect refusing to make a prediction. The distribution for these cases suggests they were justified, because the children in those categories were evenly divided between those who remained in care and those who were discharged. If one omits these cases, one is left with 305 children for whom workers were able to make a relatively strong prediction in either direction. In the two left-hand columns of the table are 60 children for whom the workers predicted little or no chance of discharge but who nevertheless left the system. In the upper right hand column are 40 children whose Time 1 workers thought they stood a good or strong

TABLE 7.31

Time 2 Worker's Prediction of Return Home and Placement Status at Five Years (N = 356) [a]

	No Chance (N = 70)	Slight Chance (N = 108)	Some Chance (N = 30)	Fair Chance (N = 76)	Good Chance (N = 30)	Strong Chance (N = 42)
Status	%	%	%	%	%	%
In Care	79	69	57	60	27	21
Discharged	21	31	43	40	73	79
	100	100	100	100	100	100

[a] Chi-square = 53.565; significant under .001 with 5 df.

chance of going home but who nevertheless remained in care. This indicates that 100 predictions out of 305 (or 33 percent) proved to be incorrect. It is noteworthy that the first type of error is greater (38 percent) than the second (27 percent), implying that workers were more pessimistic about the chances that these children would return home than later proved to be justified.

Since Time 1 workers labored, as was noted, under the most adverse conditions, one can ask whether the Time 2 workers, with the benefit of greater knowledge of the family, did any better. Table 7.32 indicates that they did.

Again, if we look at the two extreme categories, there are 48 cases in which Time 2 workers saw little or no chance of discharge where the

TABLE 7.32

Time 3 Worker's Prediction of Return Home and Placement Status at Five Years (N = 270) [a]

Status	No Chance (N = 119) %	Slight Chance (N = 54) %	Some Chance (N = 19) %	Fair Chance (N = 33) %	Good Chance (N = 16) %	Strong Chance (N = 29) %
In Care	91	80	90	79	50	38
Discharged	9	20	10	21	50	62
	100	100	100	100	100	100

[a] Chi-aquare = 48.588; significant under .001 with 5 df.

children actually were sent home. At the other extreme are 17 children for whom Time 2 workers predicted discharge but who nevertheless remained in care. Thus 65 predictions out of the 250 in which the workers went "out on a limb" (26 percent) proved inaccurate. Again the error is greater in predicting continuity of care (27 percent) than in predicting discharge (23 percent) but the gap between the two types of error is smaller.

The predictions of the Time 3 workers—occurring as they do after the children were relatively settled in placement and when those discharged were fewer in number—were less meaningful. But it is still worth noting that of 173 children whom Time 3 workers saw as having no chance of being discharged (three years after placement), 22 (or 12 percent) actually were discharged by the time the five-year span of the study was completed.

It is difficult to say whether the "errors" at the positive end of the scale are true errors, since workers predicting a good possibility of discharge when the child had been in care for over three years were not necessarily expecting it to happen by the fifth year. However, half the children for whom discharge chances were thought to be "good" were still in care at five years, and the same was true for a third of those given a "strong chance." This suggests that workers were now being somewhat over-optimistic.

The changes in the later cycles in the workers' capacity to predict do not offset the fact that it is the first-year workers' attitudes—as reflected in their predictions—that are most significant, since it is they who are the most involved in the key intake decisions. The pattern seen supports the suspicion that family capacities are underestimated and that there is a predisposition in the child welfare system to absorb the children into the system rather than to help get them out.

Summary

The workers' attitudes toward the mother had a significant influence on the decision to discharge a child from foster care at each of the four time cycles. At Times 1 and 2, the workers' attitude was as important in relation to discharge as that of the "service assets" discussed in the previous chapter. In the later stages of placement, workers' attitudes continued to be important while the influence of service assets diminished. At Time 3, however, the mother's determination to have her child discharged superseded the workers' evaluation in its influence on discharge. The worker's evaluation of the mother predicted discharge at the succeeding time cycle as well as the current one. Workers' attitudes toward children, on the other hand, played little or no role in the decision to discharge at any point in time.

Other variables influenced discharge at different times. Children placed because their mothers were physically ill were more likely than others to be discharged within the first year of placement. Children placed for alleged neglect were more likely than others to be discharged after two years. Also at this time, children were more likely to leave institutional care than foster homes and non-Catholic than agencies.

After three years in care, children placed for emotional disturbance were more likely than others to be discharged, as were white children.

At Time 4, only the worker's evaluation of the mother explained any significant degree of variance in relation to discharge.

At each time, the workers's attitude toward the mother predicted her perception of improvement, not only at the same time but for the succeeding time cycles, when the judgment of improvement was relatively independent of the evaluation.

The worker's perception of improvement was related to the mother's emotional state at Time 1. Workers were more likely to see improvement where the mother had been described as mentally ill or, at the other extreme, where she was perceived as emotionally normal. Improvement was also less likely to be seen in the first year of placement if the child was in a long-term institutional setting than in any other setting.

The total absence of the father or, at the other extreme, frequent contact at Time 1 predicted improvement in the mother at Time 2. Mothers on public assistance at Time 1 were also more likely to be seen as improved at Time 2. Economic improvement at Time 3 predicted improvement in the family at Time 4. At Time 4, mothers who visited frequently were also relatively more likely to be seen as improved.

The workers' perception of improvement in chidren was related at Time 1 to their initial evaluation of the child and to the extent to which he was considered appealing. At Time 2, workers saw improvement mainly in children whose emotional problems centered specifically around placement. Improvement was also more likely to be perceived if the child was in the care of a voluntary agency or if he was in a foster home.

At Time 3, the workers' perceptions of improvement in the child were closely related to reports of school behavior. A positive evaluation of the mother also predicted improvement in the child.

At Time 4, improvement in the child was associated with the absence of school difficulties, acceptance of placement, and involvement in a close relationship with a caseworker.

An examination of the accuracy of workers' predictions in relation to the actual status of the child suggested that the first-year workers—those most responsible for the key decisions—had an error rate of 35 to 40 percent, mostly in the direction of pessimism about the possibility of discharge.

Summary of Parts I and II

This chapter completes the report of findings in this study of agency investment. The next part of this book will deal with a substudy of agency workers that grew out of the main study. The final chapter will attempt to pull together and discuss the implications of both sets of findings. Before going on to this material, however, the key findings of the main study may be summarized as follows:

The objective of the study was to examine the impact of agency investment on children in foster care and their families. The workers, whose efforts represent the agency's major investment, were typically young, untrained, with about two years of experience, unspecialized, working under conditions of pressure, and deriving satisfaction from their work largely on the basis of direct contact with children. Over the five-year span of the study, the service assets of training, experience, and working conditions improved somewhat, but subjective feelings of dissatisfaction remained constant. Satisfactions derived from working with families declined sharply over time.

The majority of the families these workers dealt with consisted of young mothers, who were single or separated from their husbands; the women were most likely nonwhite, of low socioeconomic origins, and their children, who had been placed as a result of different types of crisis, remained in care largely because of the workers' uncertainty that these mothers could assume the full responsibility of parenthood. Contact with family other than the mother declined over time, as did frequency of contact with and positive evaluations of the mother. The picture that has emerged is generally one of deterioration and decline.

The children, on the other hand, were evaluated by their workers as healthy, developing normally, and relatively free of major emotional disturbance. The frequency of positive evaluations remained constant until the final year of the study, when the incidence of perceived emotional disturbance increased. This pattern implies that most children were seen as resilient enough to tolerate both the crises precipitated by placement and a three- to four-year experience in foster care. After that length of time, continued placement is apparently more than most children can successfully tolerate.

The workers' evaluations of the placement experience were a mixture of positives and negatives. At the end of the five-year period covered by the study, two-thirds of the children had returned home. Most discharges took place by agreement with the agency and most children and families were seen as having benefited from the experience, or were at least unharmed by it. Nevertheless, about a quarter of all discharges were considered questionable, and the experience harmful to the child, the parent, or both.

In an examination of some of the factors associated with the discharge rate, it was discovered that a relatively high rate of investment on the part of the agencies—as reflected by frequency of contact, low case loads, relative experience, and stability—strongly influenced the discharge rate in the first two years of placement, but that the significance of these factors declined later. These service assets also contributed to the perception of improvement in the child and in the mother but, in the latter case, only in the earlier phase of placement.

The worker's attitude toward the mother influenced the discharge rate at all times. It was equal in significance to the service assets in the early years and remained important while the influence of the latter declined. In the third year of placement, the mother's determination to have her child superseded the worker's evaluation. The reasons for placement and some organizational factors play a role in discharge at some times, but none of the family or agency variables examined was so influential as the worker's attitudes toward the mother in achieving the goal of return to the family.

PART THREE

A SUBSTUDY OF CHILD WELFARE WORKERS

chapter eight

CHILD WELFARE WORKERS: DESIGN OF A SUBSTUDY AND DESCRIPTION OF THE SAMPLE

T HE CONDITIONS under which data were collected during the Time 1 period of the main study inevitably raised questions about worker reactions, charged as they were with critical decisions about children and their families. As the earlier chapters have indicated, workers were predominantly young beginners, without professional training and prone to changing their jobs after relatively short periods of involvement with their clients. That their training and their experience, their stability and their attitudes, have an impact on the client's ability to leave the system has been demonstrated in the preceding chapters. Part III is a presentation of a study of the experiences of a sample of workers who were involved in the parent study. A description of the design of the study and the characteristics of the sample will be presented in this chapter. Chapter 9 will be devoted to a description of the relationship between workers' characteristics, and their mobility, their professional degree, and their impact on clients. Chapter 10 presents data which describe the differences between workers who serve in the public sector and those in the voluntary sector.[1]

Part III was written in collaboration with William Meezan, who served as research assistant for the substudy and is now research associate at the Child Welfare League of America.
1. Some of the findings in this section were reported by the author in "Occupational Mobility and Child Welfare Workers: An Exploratory Study," in *Child Welfare* 53, no. 1 (January 1974):, and in "Professional Training and the Child Welfare Worker: An Exploratory Study" in *Approaches to Innovation in Social Work Education* (New York: Council on Social Work Education, 1974).

Long before the findings of the parent study were available, strains felt by the workers were much in evidence, especially among the workers active in the critical first year, in the public agency's intake department, or in the city's shelters. Workers repeatedly used the research interview to "ventilate." They described the pressures under which they worked, their lack of satisfaction, and what they considered to be the destructiveness of the "system" to the child and the family. With the stimulus provided by this material, a study was designed to answer questions about the impact of this experience on the careers of workers affected, at least within the scope of a three-year time span from the time when they were interviewed about at least one of the study subjects to the time when they were interviewed about the nature of their work. Some of the questions raised were: to what extent were these young people's work experiences so disappointing that they were impelled to leave their field—either social work in general or child welfare in particular? To what extent would their experiences act as a form of pressure toward a full professional education?

The substudy was justified both by the magnitude of the problems involved and the absence of studies directly related to the questions asked. In the relatively short history of social work, the problems of adequate staff have apparently always been of major concern, both qualitatively and quantitatively. During the 1950s, a decade in which the number of persons holding social work positions increased by 42 percent, the proportion of those trained for the field rose by only 5 percent—from 16 percent in 1950 to 21 percent in 1960.[2] A 1968 estimate for the child welfare field raised the proportion to 25 percent.[3] As this is being written, an economic recession and the lack of government support for the poverty programs initiated in the 1960s has superficially diminished the problem by reducing the number of positions available. Nevertheless, the crucial problem of staff inadequately trained for the functions it must perform remains simply there, like Mt. Everest. Changes in the larger society affect the degree of concern, but the problem does not seem to be genuinely diminished.

Although untrained or partially trained workers constitute about 75

2. Arnulf Pins, "The Number, Size, Output, and Programs of Schools of Social Work and the Need for Professional Manpower: Implications for Expansion of Graduate Social Work Education," in *Social Work Education and Social Welfare Manpower* (New York: Council on Social Work Education, 1965).
3. David Fanshel, "Child Welfare," *Encyclopedia of Social Work*, vol. 1 (New York: National Association of Social Workers), p. 100.

percent of all those who hold social work positions, no manpower study has taken a systematic look at this group. A handful of studies to date have focused on college students in the process of making career choices, on graduate students in schools of social work, or on professional membership organizations such as the National Association of Social Workers. The "BA" workers (degree-holders without a social work major, who are not in graduate school and not eligible for membership in organizations requiring a professional degree, but who are fully involved in the field and constitute, in many ways, a critical group of toilers in the social work vineyard) have yet to be the subject of any major study.

One recent study indicated that 69 percent of the students in schools of social work enter with prior paid experience in the field,[4] but no one knows what percentage of those working in the field eventually make a permanent commitment to it in the form of graduate study. Nor does anyone know the extent to which exposure to the labyrinthian problems confronting social workers in the field acts as a deterrent to further involvement or the extent to which agencies are effective recruiters for the profession.

That there are few studies of this major source of manpower is not surprising, since the population in question is widely scattered among a broad range of agencies and cannot be identified by membership in any particular organization. In fact, the identification and description of the BA worker either in the social work field as a whole or the child welfare field in particular would be a major study in itself.

The problem of turnover has also received relatively little systematic study, even though it has long been acknowledged as a major source of strain in the field. The single major study of this problem, made by William Tollen in 1958, showed a 27 percent annual loss to child welfare agencies.[5] Even so, a survey of the manpower literature suggests that turnover has been a secondary rather than a central concern for social work. Most discussions of the manpower problem, as well as the handful of research projects in this area, have focused on recruitment (or "how to get them in"), on education (or "how to get them trained") and, more recently, on differential use of manpower (or "how to modify their func-

---

4. Deborah Golden, Arnulf Pins, Wyatt Jones, *Students in Schools of Social Work* (New York: Council on Social Work Education, 1972), page 60.
5. William Tollen, *Study of Staff Losses in Child Welfare and Family Service Agencies* (Washington, D.C.: U.S. Department of Health, Education, and Welfare, 1960).

tions so that the trained can be better used and the untrained hired").
The question of turnover (or "how to persuade them to stay where they
are") seems to come in a poor fourth in relation to the other problems; it
is usually mentioned incidentally or not at all.

It is apparently assumed that turnover is a byproduct of inadequate
recruitment and inappropriate use of personnel. A large number of va-
cancies obviously give workers considerable leeway to change jobs while
poor or inappropriate use of personnel creates some of the dissatisfaction
motivating them to change. If and when they are found, the solutions to
these presumably more basic problems are expected to solve or at least
substantially reduce the turnover problem.

Admittedly, turnover has its functional as well as its dysfunctional
aspects; change means "new blood" for the agency and broader experience for the worker. There is little doubt, however, that too much
change is dysfunctional for the agency and certainly for the client (as was
demonstrated in chapter 6) and may not always be constructive for the
worker. Although it is difficult to specify the precise level at which turnover becomes dysfunctional, it is a safe assumption that an annual rate of
27 percent, or one worker in four, would be assessed by most concerned
professionals as too high for comfort.

Exploratory Phase

The exploratory work done to develop the design of the study involved a
review of the literature, covering relevant occupational sociology as well
as the child welfare field, a review of the findings related to the workers in
the Time 1 sample of the main study, and a content analysis of their
spontaneous comments. On the basis of these materials, a working paper
was written. It presented a series of hypotheses developed in the framework of a "push-pull" analysis, which defined some of the factors expected to "pull" the beginner into the field toward full professionalization
and those which might be expected to "push" her out.

The preliminary exploration served to identify key variables, which
could be relevant to the outcomes with which the study was concerned.
These outcomes could be placed into seven categories ranging from the
most dysfunctional to the most functional: (1) leaving a child welfare
position with no intention of returning to any position in social work, (2)
leaving a child welfare position with no intention of returning to child

welfare but possibly of returning to another social work field, (3) leaving in a state of uncertainty as to whether to return to child welfare or any social work field, (4) leaving with an interest in returning but unable to do so for the foreseeable future, (5) continuing employment in child welfare but with no intention of obtaining a professional degree, (6) continuing in the field, with professional training in process but inclined to change to another field of social work, (7) continuing in the field with full professional training in process or completed but with the intention of remaining in child welfare. It is evident that the first outcome is clearly dysfunctional for the field as a whole, while the second is dysfunctional for child welfare. The third, fourth, and fifth are marginal, that is, favorable in some respects and unfavorable in others. The sixth outcome is functional for the field of social work but not for child welfare, while the seventh one is the most clearly favorable for the child welfare field.

The variables seen as potentially important included such demographic factors as age, sex, race, marital status, socioeconomic status, and social mobility. They also included personality factors and social or ideological values. Working conditions, expectations, and satisfactions derived from the work done were also expected to be important in achieving a degree or in changing jobs.

Among the variables expected to push the worker out of the field were relative youth, being male, being married, and personal maladjustment. Among work-related variables were the absence of preexisting career goals or career goals related to other professions, while among attitudinal variables were ambiguity and confusion about the nature of the work role, the lack of recognition for untrained workers, low salaries, and the perception of earning powers as lower than that of one's peers.

Among the variables expected to pull workers into the field were prior experience in related fields, accurate pre-entry information, relatively strong confidence in the value of the work done, ability to come to terms with deviant client behavior, a strong client-orientation, and the ability to use informal methods to achieve desirable goals. The provision of adequate in-service training, the perception of the supervisor as a role model and of the administration as a supportive power, and a high level of peer group support were also expected to contribute to workers' decisions to make a full career commitment.

Reflection about the possible effects of some variables led to the conclusion that their influence was likely to be bimodal (producing responses related to one extreme or the other). It was expected that strong convictions about the need for social change would serve either as a push (for those who conclude that social work is not productive) or as a pull (for those who feel that social work is constructive or could become so and want to be better qualified). The absence of such convictions was expected to lead to a marginal outcome, such as remaining in the field without obtaining a degree. On the other hand, convictions about the value of placement as a method of service were seen as leading to the same marginal outcome while lack of conviction about its value would either lead the worker to leave the field or to further training in search of more satisfactory forms of service. On a more material level, the ability to tolerate uncomfortable working conditions and heavy case loads was also seen as permitting the worker to remain in his marginal role of a BA worker while intolerance for such discomfort might lead either to the extreme of leaving the field or to that of completing training and, through that, of achieving more comfortable work.

Relevant Theory

In contrast to the main study, which was concerned with the relationship of an entire network of agencies to its clients, the substudy centered on a single occupational role. It was therefore easier to identify some theoretical formulations which could be tested in the framework of the substudy. Most of these formulations came from Blau's studies of public assistance workers. In one of these,[6] Blau noted that a typical reaction of the inexperienced worker was surprise to learn that clients lied, did not express gratitude, and had "low morals." Child welfare workers, particularly those in public agencies, frequently encounter the most extreme and socially unacceptable forms of psychopathology: drug addiction, sexual deviations, promiscuity, prostitution, chronic alcoholism, criminal activity, incest, and severe physical abuse of children. Most of this is seen in connection with natural parents, but there is also much in the behavior of adolescent and preadolescent children that comes under the heading of what Blau termed "reality shock": precocious sexuality, obscene language, destructiveness, the ability to manipulate others. This led to the formulation of the hypothesis that the ability to survive "reality shock" or

6. Peter Blau, "Orientation Toward Clients in a Public Welfare Agency," *Administrative Science Quarterly* 5 (December 1960): 341–61.

to tolerate social deviance among clients increased the likelihood of the kind of outcomes classed as favorable in this study.

Another of Blau's studies [7] suggested that peer relations may be a more significant influence on worker decisions than is commonly appreciated in the field. Blau studied the extent to which colleagues respected one another and consulted each other, as did procedure-oriented workers. This led to the hypothesis that having an orientation in common with one's colleagues acts as a pull toward a favorable outcome.

More important for this study were the concepts of client-orientation and procedure-orientation in themselves. Blau described "client-oriented workers" as those who were more concerned with giving service than with the efficient operation of the agency. They disapproved of "restricting service to clients and merely checking their eligibility." On the other hand, procedure-oriented workers were concerned with efficiency and "disapproved of wasting time and furnishing more extensive service to clients than a strict interpretation of the rules required." [8]

This philosophical dichotomy is probably observable to some degree in most agencies. Since social work training is, in effect, directed toward strengthening the client-orientation, it is likely that it is most observable in agencies where the level of professional training is low. In the context of this study, it was hypothesized that the stronger the client-orientation, the greater the likelihood of a favorable outcome in terms of professionalization. These workers may be dissatisfied with the particular agency by which they are employed, but it seems unlikely that they will reject the whole field. If anything, the urge to complete training and qualify for employment with agencies with higher standards would probably be strongest among the client-oriented. On the other hand, the worker who is oriented to procedures would not necessarily be pushed out of the field, but would be more likely to continue employment without making the effort to achieve a professional degree. If neither orientation dominated, it seemed likely that the worker would leave the field—since lack of clear orientation in either direction suggested either indifference or an inability to resolve the conflicts inherent in the social worker's function.

Another concept identified in the literature and used in the study was

7. Peter Blau, "Patterns of Choice on Interpersonal Relations, *American Sociological Review*, 27, no. 1 (February 1962): 41–55.
8. Blau, *ibid.*, p. 49.

that of "role deprivation," which refers to the ability of the worker to make choices and order priorities in carrying out assigned tasks. Billingsley, who studied work patterns in a child protective agency and in a family service setting, found that performance patterns were significantly different: workers in the family counseling agency spent their time with clients in the office, while workers in the child protective agency divided their time between clients and the community; yet both preferred to concentrate on clients. The latter group was then said to suffer a greater degree of "role deprivation" than the former.[9]

Evidence from the main study indicated that "deprivation" in the sense described by Billingsley was very much present among the workers in question. It was hypothesized that the greater the deprivation, the greater the likelihood of a polarized response; i.e., some workers might be pushed out of the field by such deprivation, while others might apply for admission to professional school in order to be eligible for positions where they would be less deprived. Again, the workers for whom this form of discomfort is minimal would be more likely to work without professional training.

Sample Selection

Of the 511 workers interviewed at Time 1 in the parent study, 70 were eliminated because they had a Master's Degree and 10 because they were members of religious orders. The workers reached for the substudy interview totaled 222, or approximately 50 percent of those eligible. The largest part of the response problem was attributable to the high mobility of the study population, since most of the nonrespondents were those whose current whereabouts could not be traced beyond the geographic limits of the interviewing staff, which was confined to interview locations within one day's travel from New York City.

One major source of difficulty stemmed from the fact that the study population was largely young and female. Many of the workers who were not traced may have married after leaving the agency and could not have been reached unless their married names were known to the agency.

As expected, employer agencies were the main source of information about the subjects' current whereabouts. When letters sent to the address given by the agency were returned, the worker was traced through the use

9. Andrew Billingsley, "The Role of the Social Worker in a Child Protective Agency," *Child Welfare* 43, no. 9 (November 1964): 472–79.

of the telephone directory, through clues provided by the interview in the parent study, and through letters to schools of social work in the New York area. This last resource was particularly helpful; the schools located more than 40 respondents.

Other reasons for lack of response were unclear. Some agencies gave information only about workers still in their employ. One of the agencies that did not send information had registered objections to the collection of data about staff during the first year of the main study and was not involved in its later phases. The data collection period was extended four months beyond the original deadline in an effort to reach hard-core nonrespondents; this extension did not substantially raise the response rate.

Since data were available from the main sample, systematic comparisons were possible between respondents and nonrespondents on 29 variables. There were no significant differences with respect to such basic population figures as age, sex, race, or marital status, or to such work-related items as training and experience. There were only three statistically significant differences, all on attitudinal terms. In examining these differences and those showing trends which verged on statistical significance, the indications were that the sample loss occurred in the direction of the workers least committed to the field—that is, the youngest age group, the case aides with no social work training or plans for training, and those who were annoyed by such bureaucratic problems as demands for recoding but were not disturbed by the lack of supervision.

The most important difference, however, was the underrepresentation of workers from voluntary agencies; 48 percent of the voluntary-agency workers eligible for the study were reached, in contrast to 60 percent of the public-agency workers. As will be seen later, when the findings on mobility are reported, public-agency workers tended to transfer to other departments within their very large agency. This made them easier to trace than the voluntary-agency workers, who had less opportunity to transfer when dissatisfied with their positions and were more likely to resign.

Data Collection and Analysis

The principal instrument used in the substudy was a semistructured tape-recorded interview, which took approximately two hours to complete, usually in one session. The interview covered the respondent's occupational history, other careers considered, and how she came to take a position in social work. Respondents were asked for descriptions of the agencies where they worked, their structure, agency atmosphere, relationships with supervisors, colleagues, etc. They were also asked for descriptions of their case loads and to discuss their problems and their satisfactions with working with their clients. The extent to which they were involved with other agencies was also explored, as were their general views on the child welfare system.

Most subjects were conscientious respondents and answered questions fully and informatively. Three percent were reported by the interviewers to be exceptionally difficult subjects, while 20 percent were rated as "somewhat difficult." Open or even subtle hostility, marked evasion, or defensiveness were rare. Some areas expected to be sensitive proved not to be, but a few questions were difficult to express in a form whose meaning was clear to the respondents. Only one respondent objected to the use of the tape recorder. No objections were registered by any of the agencies represented, either in relation to procedures or to the contents of the schedule. The interview data were supplemented by a questionnaire—designed primarily to tap attitudes not covered by the interview. It was left with the respondent, to be filled out and mailed as soon as possible after the interview. The questionnaire was completed by 177 of the workers interviewed, which is a response rate of 80 percent.

Most interviews took place during working hours in the respondent's office. All interviewing was done by trained professionals with master's degrees in social work or equivalent experience. Most of them had previously been employed as interviewers for the main study. Ten were involved, five of whom were active throughout the period of data collection. Efforts were made to match respondents by race and sex wherever possible.

After the interviews were completed, interviewers filled out a precoded schedule while listening to a playback, a process which saved on recording and transcription time. The completed schedule was reviewed by the research staff, who dealt with coding problems encountered by the interviewers. A 10 percent reliability check on the precoded schedule showed an agreement rate of 85 percent.

Fifteen decks of data were coded, placed on tape, and processed through the use of Harvard Data-Text Programs on the IBM 360 at Columbia University's Computer Center. To test most of the hypotheses formulated in the exploratory phase of the study, indices were developed.

Interview data and questionnaire items were entered into the Data-Text correlation program, which uses the Pearson *r*. The results indicated that most of the original hypotheses could be measured by an index that was adequate in terms of the magnitude of the intercorrelations among the items, the number of items, and the degree of internal consistency as measured by the Cronbach Alpha. The development of some indices led to the reformulation of some of the original hypotheses and the addition of some new ones. The analysis then followed the same pattern as that of the main study. All potentially significant variables were cross-tabulated against the outcomes with which the study was concerned. To determine whether the significant variables were interrelated, a regression analysis was done. The content of these indices will be discussed in the description of the study sample and in connection with the findings presented in chapters 9 and 10.

Findings: An Overview of the Study Sample

Demographic Characteristics

The substudy sample was, like the sample of workers in the main study, heavily female (77 percent), white (78 percent), and relatively young (the mean age was 32). Of the workers sampled, 56 percent were or had been employed by a public child welfare agency, the remaining 44 percent by voluntary agencies.

The sample was about evenly divided between those who were currently married and those who were single or no longer married; 40 percent had children. In religious preference, 31 percent were Catholics, 26 percent were Jewish, and 19 percent were Protestant; the remaining 24 percent were either unaffiliated or members of other religious groups. Nearly half were stable in terms of socioeconomic status, since their fathers were or had been professionals or white collar workers (44 percent) or had at least completed high school (43 percent). The rest were upwardly mobile; their own status as college graduates in a professional occupation was superior to that of their fathers.

At the beginning of the period covered by the interview (1966), the large majority (82 percent) were earning salaries under $8,000 a year. By the time of the interview (1970), the majority were well past this level, with the highest group (22 percent) reporting earnings in the $11,000 to $14,000 range.

Respondents were interviewed, on the average, approximately three and a half years after their initial contact with the main body. Since most had had a year or two of experience at the time of the first contact, the data obtained typically describe the first four or five years of a career in social work for those who continued in the field and a two- to three-year work experience for those who did not.

The changes in the status of these workers with respect to education and employment between the two interviews are described in Table 8.1.

TABLE 8.1

Training Status and Occupational Changes (N = 222)

Educational Status	%	Occupational Changes	%
BA in 1966; unchanged in 1970	34	1966 position un-	
Partially trained; unchanged	18	changed	19
Training for other fields;		On leave of absence	9
unchanged	10	Same agency; different	
BA in 1966; completed MSW	11	position	36
Partial training; com-		Different child	
pleted MSW	10	welfare agency	3
BA; partial training	9	Different social	
Training for other fields		work position in	
in 1966; changed to social		non–child welfare	
work training in 1970	6	field	13
BA or partial training in		Non–social work oc-	
social work; changed to		cupations	8
another field	2	Not employed	12
	100		100

As Table 8.1 indicates, 34 percent were untrained at the time of the initial contact and were still untrained as social workers when they were interviewed. A total of 33 percent had partial training but did not yet have an MSW, while 21 percent had received one. The remaining 12 percent were working toward or had received degrees in other fields. When the first three categories were combined, the figures indicated that 62 percent of the respondents held a position in relation to social work training which remained unchanged during the period covered. Of those who did make some change, the largest group was the one that had obtained a social work degree. Nearly all the rest had begun or were continuing training, while only a few had embarked on careers in other fields. What is perhaps most striking is the large number who made no move in the direction of training at an age which, for the majority, was the optimal time to do so.

When the first three categories in the occupational change part of the table were combined, it appeared that 64 percent of the respondents remained at least formally affiliated with their original employer, but the proportion of those who changed their status within the agency was almost double those who were stable. It should be noted, however, that the largest group—those who transferred to other departments—was inflated somewhat by the fact that the public agency closed one division during the period covered, assigning most of its workers to other child welfare departments.

When the group at home was combined with those in unrelated occupations, indications were that at least 20 percent of the respondents were lost to social work for the foreseeable future. When this group was combined with those in other social work positions, the loss to the child welfare field was 33 percent.

That only 12 percent were out of the work force and at home was surprising for a largely young, heavily female sample. This may be a product of sample bias, since a potential respondent whose married name was not known to the agency would have presented more tracing problems than others, but the low proportion may also be a sign of the times. Considering the decline in the birth rate, the impact of the women's liberation movement, and an economic recession compelling many married women to work, it is likely that the proportion of workers staying home with their families was smaller than it would have been had the study been done five years earlier.

Occupational History

Fully 87 percent of the respondents had given serious consideration to at least one career other than social work, and most of these had considered more than one; 56 percent did not make a serious career choice until college or afterward. One-third had made a choice before entering college but, at the other extreme, 10 percent still had not reached such a decision at the time they were interviewed. Social work was the initial career choice for only 23 percent of the respondents. First choices were most likely to be in service fields, such as nursing or teaching (36 percent of the sample). While the variety of first choices was fairly diverse, it is also noteworthy that only 21 percent initially chose non-service careers.

Reasons for changing to social work were about equally balanced between the positive (social work was seen as more satisfying than the initial choice) and the negative (inability to succeed in the field of choice).

Twenty-four percent said they had moved away from their initial choice because they were attracted by the "helping" content of social work, but a similar proportion reported that they had turned to social work after having decided that they were not suited to their first choice. An additional 17 percent were dissatisfied with the work they were doing while 11 percent had problems meeting the requirements for graduate work in their preferred fields.

Consistent with this picture of social work as a second choice is the fact that it was not the first field of employment either; 57 percent of the respondents had held a position in another field of employment before they entered social work. Surprisingly enough for a relatively young population, 17 percent had been employed in at least two other fields before entering social work.

Also consistent with this picture of relatively late interest is that 42 percent reported having a positive image of social workers before their own entry into the field. A quarter reported a clearly negative image and 34 percent had only a vague image or could not describe any image at all to the interviewer. Those who reported positive images of social workers saw them as "helping," "warm," or "giving" people, who were doing important and meaningful work. Of those who had negative images, the most commonly reported was that of the "Lady Bountiful do-gooder." These workers also perceived social workers as old, naive ("didn't know anything about reality"), incompetent ("those who stayed in welfare work couldn't find anything else to do," "inept at what they were doing, using language and jargon no one understood"), disturbed ("sick people handling sick people," "frustrated old maids"), irrelevant ("the whole society stinks and the social worker tries to put on a Band-Aid"), as well as the proverbial drab appearance ("long skirt, oxford shoes, carrying a basket," "old ladies with stack heels").

"Significant others" seemed to have played a strong role in influencing the workers in this sample to enter the field: 35 percent reported being influenced by friends or relatives who were social workers themselves, 14 percent reported the same positive influence from teachers, while 9 percent were influenced by members of the family not in the field. Negative influences or pressure not to enter social work was exerted upon only 6 percent of the respondents, usually by members of the family not in the field.

For most respondents (58 percent), the attraction of the field lay in the opportunity to work with people. Only 10 percent pointed to material benefits such as salary or the security of a civil service position. For those giving other reasons, fully 26 percent said that social work had no positive attraction for them beyond the fact that a job was available and it was expedient to accept it. Slightly over half said they had no alternative for employment at the time they took the position.

The largest group of respondents (38 percent) found their positions through friends while only 25 percent found employment through employment agencies or advertisements, suggesting that there may be a greater degree of informal recruiting from within the profession than is generally acknowledged. The remainder found their jobs as a result of general knowledge acquired from various sources such as announcements of civil service examinations.

Most of the respondents felt no strong commitment to the field at the time of their initial contact with the main study but, by the time they were interviewed for the substudy, their feelings had changed considerably. In retrospect, only 14 percent saw themselves as already fully committed to social work when they entered the field while 28 percent thought they had been fairly certain of their commitment. Twenty percent were then trying to choose between social work and another career while 35 percent considered themselves uncommitted to any career. As of the time of the interview for the substudy, 37 percent of those continuing in social work considered themselves fully committed, 36 percent were fairly certain of their commitment but still had some reservations, while the proportion still uncommitted to any career declined to 27 percent.

Physical Conditions

As was anticipated, a considerable degree of discomfort was reported in virtually all the areas covered by the interview, ranging from the immediate physical aspects of the work to general assessments of the social value of the work being done. Most of the workers shared their offices and their telephones. Over half reported sharing offices with more than six people. Common complaints were lack of privacy for interviewing, crowding, noise, lack of secretarial service, and inadequate equipment for recording. Half the respondents reported that arrangements to permit privacy in interviewing were inadequate. Slightly less than half reported that they maintained case records only when absolutely necessary or only sporadically. Field travel was the only area covered under the heading of physical working conditions which the majority did not find problematic. At the very least, workers did not mind this aspect of their jobs while many saw it in a positive light—constructive for their objectives, and providing relief from office tension.

Salaries

Since, as reported earlier, the salaries for most positions fell within the relatively narrow range of $6,000–$8,000 a year, an effort to gauge the effects of earning powers was based on questions related to the deprivations felt by the respondents when they compared themselves to their peers. When asked to compare their salaries to those of their friends, 41 percent reported they were earning less, 25 percent thought they were earning about the same, while only 21 percent thought they were earning more; the remaining 13 percent gave a mixed response or could not make such a comparison. The majority denied feeling that the difference affected them, although more than a third felt that their jobs made heavier demands. On the other hand, 51 percent saw themselves as more satisfied with their work than their friends were, a factor which may have compensated somewhat for their relatively low earnings.

Information

Forty-three percent felt that initially they had been poorly informed about the nature of their work and found it considerably different from their expectations, 30 percent described the level of information they had as neither poor or good, leaving only 27 percent who felt that initially they had been well informed about the work they were undertaking. The most frequently named areas of misinformation referred to the nature of the job itself (the type of casework done or the lack of it, lack of direct contact with children, etc.), agency structure (such as the degree of bureaucratic rigidity), and, less frequently, the nature of the client population.

Staff

The general level of professionalism encountered by most respondents was low. The large majority (80 percent) reported that all or most of their peers were untrained workers like themselves. More than half, however, reported that some or most of their colleagues were working toward a professional degree in social work. Only one-third reported that all supervisors in their agencies were trained. Their own supervisors were about evenly divided between those who had MSWs and those who did not. Nearly half reported that all holders of master's degrees in their agencies were supervisors, executives, or consultants.

Training

With reference to in-service training, 33 percent reported that they were trained solely through individual conferences with their supervisors. The majority reported orientation meetings or separate training units, usually in combination with supervisory sessions. Such training was apparently confined to the first few months of employment, since most workers reported that training was continued only through sessions with supervisors: attendance at seminars or professional meetings or time off for courses was rare.

The sample was about equally divided between those who considered their training adequate and those who did not. Among those who were dissatisfied, the most common complaint was the training sessions' lack of relevance for their actual functions.

Supervision

The large majority (84 percent) reported having more than one supervisor even during the relatively short time period covered in the study. Despite the instability, and the uneven professional level of supervision given, most workers were apparently supervised quite closely; 41 percent reported that they saw their supervisors on a weekly basis and had additional time with them as needed. Only 10 percent reported that contact with supervisors occurred only occasionally.

Supervision was almost always carried out in the formal context of meetings. Most workers (62 percent) reported that informal contact with supervisors was a rare or only an occasional occurrence. What informal contacts there were took the form of casual conversations "in passing." As one worker commented, "coffee breaks with the supervisor were exceptions, not the rule. Supervisors had their own peer groups."

Despite these seemingly negative features of supervision, the respondents' evaluation of the quality of their supervison was more likely to be positive than negative. Of the workers, 63 percent thought their supervisors were always or usually helpful, 26 percent found their supervisors only occasionally or rarely helpful, and the remainder indicated that helpfulness varied with the case discussed. The most commonly named areas of helpfulness were defined as implementing casework skills and adding to the worker's general knowledge of the field. When asked about the extent to which supervisors were involved in their case decisions, the largest group of respondents (50 percent) felt that their decisions were made jointly while 31 percent thought they made most decisions themselves. Only 19 percent felt that the supervisors were the real decision-makers. Furthermore, nearly one-third saw their supervisors as having a positive effect on their career decisions, even though—as the findings will indicate later—the variables related to supervision showed little relationship to the actual career changes observed.

Peers

Informal interaction with fellow workers was much more common, as might be expected, than interaction with supervisors. The large majority (76 percent) reported that such interaction was frequent and usually or always informal. Half reported that consultation between workers was a common occurrence, that they themselves consulted colleagues, and that the conferences were most commonly concerned with individual cases. Somewhat less frequently, individual consultations concerned forms and procedures or general casework problems; least frequent were conferences dealing with problems in agency structure and in the utilization of outside resources. Most workers (61 percent) found such consultation often or always useful. One worker stated flatly that "nothing gets done on formal lines; if anything gets done, it's based on informal interaction." Another said, "We get most of our information from each other. . . . that's where most of the help came from."

This was not for lack of other help. Nearly all respondents had access to consultants, usually psychiatrists; but they, with only occasional exceptions, could be reached only through such formal methods as filling out forms, and wirting summaries, which usually required the supervisor's approval. Only 32 percent reported that the consultant was usually helpful while 36 percent said he was seldom or only occasionally helpful. Thirty percent of the workers in agencies employing MSWs in direct practice expressed some doubt about the appropriateness of the way the agency used its trained personnel.

Atmosphere

In reporting on agency atmosphere, 42 percent of the workers said it was very or moderately tense while only 11 percent described it as "stimulating"; 16 percent reported it varied with time, while 31 percent said it was quiet or "generally positive." Good atmosphere was most often attributed to good relations among colleagues while poor atmosphere was more likely to be attributed to overly bureaucratic procedures.

A large majority (71 percent) had only minimal or occasional contact with anyone in the agency hierarchy above their supervisors. At least one worker said that the staff was instructed not to contact anyone more than two levels above their own position. Not surprisingly, only 36 percent reported favorable attitudes toward the agency hierarchy while the remainder were either indifferent (13 percent), mildly critical (31 percent), or hostile (20 percent). The large majority (78 percent) reported that they questioned agency policy at least occasionally, either in discussions with their peers or in conferences with their supervisors. Most of the policies questioned were those which affected the clients directly rather than those which affected workers. An analysis of the areas of conflict indicated that almost half thought the agency's priorities were not what they should be. This was exemplified in such statements as "foster family care is very destructive. Of the families I supervised, only one or two were beneficial." "The agency is too anti- [natural] parent." "The system is too ready to take children away from natural families, claiming foster care is ideal and it's not." "With all the talk and conferences, nothing is really done to get a child out."

Workers claimed to be more preoccupied with their commitment to quality service, their ability to help clients, and their personal growth, while they saw the agency as being more concerned with indications of work completed, such as closing the "right" number of cases and completing a quota of interviews, than with the quality of these activities.

Case Loads

Most of the workers who counted their case loads in terms of the number of children had more than 20 while those whose statistical unit was the family usually had 16 or more. Those whose case load was defined in terms of the number of foster homes supervised typically had between 11 and 15 homes. The large majority said that these loads were typical for their agencies. Because supervisors generally assigned cases according to the workers' availability, most workers had either no choice or only an occasional choice of assignments.

The functions most commonly named by workers as part of their duties were working with natural families, obtaining histories, liaison work with other agencies, and direct work with children. Less than half the sample (43 percent) said that emergencies were a constant or frequent occurrence. In organizing their work, half the respondents said that first priority went to the emergency situation.

The most commonly mentioned routine task was paper work. Next most common was routine field visiting. More than half the respondents (53 percent) felt that the number of routine tasks, when compared to tasks initiated by the workers in the interests of the clients, was high. Most workers, however, either accepted routine tasks as a part of the job without complaint, or else defined them as a necessary evil.

Most workers were assigned both boys and girls in their case loads, but family work was done mainly with mothers. The largest proportion (37 percent) had case loads consisting mainly of clients who were black but nearly all had some white and Puerto Rican clients as well.

The client trait most frequently named as a source of satisfaction was the desire for a relationship (61 percent); conversely, the most disturbing trait was the absence of such a desire. Clients were seen as hostile, withdrawn, or unable to acknowledge their problems. Since most respondents were white, middle-class workers serving non-white, lower-class clients, they were asked to discuss the extent to which class or cultural differences were problematic for them. Of the respondents, 35 percent denied having any such problems at all, 46 percent recognized the existence of class and/or cultural differences but claimed to have resolved or minimized them in the course of their work, and 19 percent acknowledged that they were troubled by such differences. The most commonly perceived problems were differences in lifestyles (mentioned by 41 percent), language problems (32 percent), and client hostility on social or class grounds (24 percent).

Quality of Service

Worker opinion of the quality of the services their agencies rendered was fairly evenly distributed on a scale from poor to very good but was somewhat skewed in the direction of "poor." Better training for the staff was the most commonly named area in which improvement was needed. On the other hand, most workers felt that at least some of the children and some of the families benefited from the service given. The failure of families to benefit was most often attributed to the inappropriateness of the service—the fact that it was aimed at the "wrong" problem, as in cases where the need was for economic aid to the parents, rather than the manipulation of the child's environment. In relation to children, the most commonly named failure was the poor quality of service or of the facilities offered.

Continuity

Since discontent with many aspects of their work was widespread for these workers, general attitudes toward changing jobs or continuing on are significant. Of those who were continuing, satisfaction had increased over time for 38 percent and decreased for 25 percent. Of the entire group, 54 percent were as, or more, satisfied with their work than when they were hired, 29 percent were as, or more, dissatisfied, and the remainder had been continuously indifferent or neutral. Belief in the importance of their work, contact with clients, and increased competence were the most commonly named sources of satisfaction, described with about equal frequency.

Most of the 71 transfers to other departments were the result of administrative changes; 22 percent, however, transferred in order to obtain a promotion to supervisor. Only 13 percent gave dissatisfaction with their work assignments as a reason for the change.

Of those who left the agency, the largest proportion (36 percent) gave marriage or family responsibilities as the reason; 29 percent intended to return to school; 31 percent mentioned agency problems, such as salary, reorganization, or quality of service; 28 percent gave a change in interests as their reason for leaving.[10]

Of those who took other positions, 33 percent took work in a related (service) field, 20 percent took jobs in social work but not in child welfare, while only 16 percent remained in child welfare. The remaining 31 percent entered fields unrelated to social work. Not surprisingly, most of these workers said that they were satisfied with their current position, and they attributed their satisfaction either to the nature of their work or to the approach of the agency toward helping clients. Only 21 percent gave inadequate salaries as the cause of their dissatisfaction, while 16 percent mentioned the reduction in pressure, better supervision, or better learning or training opportunities.

Or those who had completed or were in the process of completing their

10. These figures total to more than 100 percent because respondents gave more than one reason.

MSWs, 65 percent were planning to continue in child welfare, but half of these were doing so because of a scholarship commitment.

Overall Assessments

As part of a series of general assessments, the respondents were asked to describe the principal satisfactions of their work. Not surprisingly, a large majority (78 percent) said they derived their satisfactions from contact with children while substantial minorities derived them from working with natural families (34 percent) or from developing their own skill (28 percent). On the other hand, their frustrations were focused on the system of services (64 percent) or the agency employing them (55 percent). Working with foster families and institutional personnel were minor sources of both satisfaction and frustration.

The most commonly named causes of frustration were the lack of services and facilities in the child welfare system (50 percent), the helplessness or the unimportance of the social worker (36 percent) and the feeling mentioned earlier that the system's priorities were wrong (36 percent).

As would be expected from the earlier pattern of responses, the majority (72 percent) considered the child welfare system to be very or generally inadequate; 43 percent thought that the system required radical or considerable change while 52 percent were somewhat more conservative and would settle for "some change." Only 5 percent thought the system needed little, if any, change.

Index Scores

It was evident that a number of hypotheses, particularly those involving worker attitudes, were better measured by the development of indices that combined the responses to a number of related items than by the use of single items. The indices described in this section are those measuring attitudes which proved significant in relation to at least one of the problems analyzed.

Personality Measures: Rejection of Authority and Tolerance for Ambiguity

As we noted earlier, it was hypothesized that personal maladjustment would be associated with an unfavorable outcome. Given the limitations of the study, the sample involved, and the limitations of paper-and-pencil personality tests, the best option was to limit personality measures to those reflecting relatively specific traits, which could be considered important for social work practice, rather than to use tests that aim for a more general assessment of personal functioning. Two such measures were identified from the literature. The first, called "Rejection of Authority" in this study, was developed by Bales and Couch [11] and consisted of a series of statements to which the respondent is asked to indicate the extent of agreement on a scale from "Strongly Disagree" to "Strongly Agree." These were incorporated into the questionnaire as follows:

AUTHORITY SCALE

1. Obedience and respect for authority are the most important virtues children should learn.
2. There is hardly anything lower than a person who does not feel great love, gratitude, and respect for his parents.
3. What youth needs most is strict discipline, rugged determination, and the will to work and fight for family and country.
4. You have to respect authority, and when you stop respecting authority, your situation is not worth much.
5. Patriotism and loyalty are the first and most important requirements for a good citizen.
6. Young people sometimes get rebellious ideas, but as they grow up, they ought to get over them and settle down.
7. A child should not be allowed to talk back to his parents or else he will lose respect for them.
8. The facts on crime and sexual immorality show that we will have to crack down harder on young people if we are going to save our moral standard.
9. Disobeying an order is one thing you cannot excuse—if one gets away with disobedience, why can't everybody?
10. A well-raised child is one who does not have to be told twice to do something.

The second personality measure was called "Tolerance for Ambiguity" for the purposes of this study and was measured by the following items

11. Described in James Bieri and Robin Lobeck, "Acceptance of Authority and Parental Identification," *Journal of Personality* 37, no. 1 (1959): 74–86.

also inserted in the questionnaire. Again, the respondents were asked to state their relative agreement.

AMBIGUITY SCALE

1. An expert who does not come up with a definite answer probably does not know too much.
2. A good job is one where what is to be done and how it is to be done are always clear.
3. What we are used to is always preferable to the unfamiliar.
4. A person who leads an even, regular life in which few surprises or unexpected happenings arise really has a lot to be grateful for.
5. The sooner we all acquire similar values and ideals, the better.
6. I would like to live in a foreign country for a while.
7. People who fit their lives to a schedule probably miss most of the joy of living.
8. Often the most interesting and stimulating people are those who do not mind being different and original.
9. Many of our most important decisions are based on insufficient information.
10. A good teacher is one who makes you wonder about your way of looking at things.

Originally called "Intolerance for Ambiguity," this scale was developed by Budner and purports to measure "the tendency of the individual to perceive ambiguous situations either as a source of threat or as a desirable state of affairs." [12] The first personality measures were justified on the grounds that the professional values of social work are most compatible with a nonauthoritarian personality pattern. "Tolerance for Ambiguity" was considered a necessary trait for workers who deal with complex human problems, not readily soluble by administrative directives. It was expected that the workers most likely to complete their professional education and remain in the field would score high on tolerance for ambiguity and also on the rejection of authority. Workers inclined to accept authority were expected to remain in their jobs without further training.

On the "Acceptance of Authority" scale, worker scores spread fairly evenly over a broad range, making it possible to place respondents on a

12. Stanley Budner, "Intolerance of Ambiguity as a Personality Variable," *Journal of Personality* 30 (1962): 29–50.

range from those with strong tendencies toward acceptance of authority to those with a marked inclination to defy or reject it. The fact that there was a relatively even distribution on this scale came as a surprise, since the experience of the main study gave the impression that the field was heavily populated by rebellious young people. The evidence of the study suggests that there were at least as many of a more compliant disposition who were evidently less visible or audible.

The scores on the "Tolerance of Ambiguity" scale were skewed in a more positive direction, with most workers indicating some ability to tolerate ambiguity. Nevertheless the range of scores was broad enough to divide the workers into three categories: those with low tolerance capacity, those with moderate capacities, and those with high capacity.

Need for Change

It was hypothesized that workers with strong convictions about the need for social change would be impelled either to leave the field out of frustration or to aim for full professional training. The absence of such convictions was expected to lead to the marginal outcome of continuing on the job without further training.

To measure this feeling, an index was developed; it included five items, of which three were responses given by the worker in the interview and two were judgments made by the interviewer:

NEED FOR CHANGE SCALE

1. Respondent's tendency to question agency policy.
2. Respondent's opinion as to the need for change in the child welfare system.
3. Respondent's opinion as to the need for change in social work as a whole.
4. Interviewer's assessment of respondent's conventionality.
5. Interviewer's assessment of respondent's ideological position.

As was indicated by the trends reported earlier, the respondents tended to score in the direction of expressing a strong need for change. Nevertheless, the group could be divided into those with low scores (indicating a tendency to accept the status quo), those with middle-range scores (suggesting mixed feelings or reservations), and those with high scores (indicating strong convictions).

Early Career Decisions

It was hypothesized that workers who had aimed for social work careers before they took the position described in the study were more likely to have favorable outcomes than those who did not. This hypothesis was measured by a two-item index consisting of workers' statements as to when their interest in social work developed and when they planned for graduate school, the earlier the interest and the plans for graduate school, the stronger the preexisting career goals were presumed to be.

Client-Procedure Orientation

To test the hypothesis mentioned earlier, that client-oriented workers would have more favorable outcomes than the procedure-oriented, measures developed by Billingsley [13] and used by Epstein [14] in other studies were incorporated in the questionnaire. These four items (6–8 in the scale below), together with three other questionnaire responses and two responses in the interview—all of which were highly correlated—constituted the measure of client-procedure orientation.

CLIENT-PROCEDURE ORIENTATION SCALE

1. Respondent's statement about the effect of agency structure on the client.
2. Respondent's attitude toward routine tasks.
3. If it will help get a child placed, a worker is justified in omitting potentially damaging information from a referral letter.
4. One cannot really blame clients for lying to get things they need.
5. Clients who want better service are justified in creating disturbances in agency offices.
6. A caseworker should act so as to meet the needs of her client, even though a particular act is considered "unprofessional" by her colleagues.
7. A caseworker should act so as to carry out the policies of the agency even if doing so differs from what her own professional judgment leads her to believe should be done.

13. Andrew Billingsley, "Bureaucratic and Professional Orientation Patterns in Social Casework," *Social Service Review*, 38, no. 4 (1964): 400–407.
14. Irwin Epstein, "Professionalization and Social Work Activism" (PhD diss., Columbia University, 1969), p. 232.

8. A caseworker should act so as to meet the needs of her client, even if a particular act differs from explicitly stated agency policies.
9. A caseworker should act so as to carry out the policies of the agency even if doing so differs with what the referral source, or other important segments of the community, think should be done.

The frequency distribution indicated that most respondents had middle-range scores, suggesting mixed views. Nevertheless it was possible to place them on a range from those closest to a procedure orientation to those most strongly client-oriented.

Adequacy of Training
The hypothesis that satisfaction with their in-service training would lead to full professional training was tested using an index composed of two statements in the interview and three questionnaire responses.

TRAINING SCALE

1. Respondent's statement about the adequacy of training.
2. Respondent's statement as to whether training was interesting.
3. Workers were well-trained by the agency for their work.
4. Staff meetings were useful.
5. Staff meeting were interesting.

Although responses tended toward the low (inadequate) end of the scale, it was still possible to categorize the respondents on a continuum from those with totally negative views of their training to those with relatively positive opionins.

"Anti-elitism"
As we noted earlier, 30 percent of the respondents expressed the opinion that workers with a master's degree in social work were not used appropriately by their agencies or that their abilities were overrated. The correlational analysis indicated that such attitudes were likely to be expressed by the same workers who agreed with the questionnaire statement that "too often psychiatrists' reports are not worth waiting for." On the index that combined these items, 59 percent of the respondents expressed some degree of feeling that could be described as "anti-elitism," that is, doubts about the usefulness of psychiatrists and trained caseworkers.

Social Deviance

The respondents' capacity to tolerate deviance in their clients was measured by an index composed of three questionnaire items:

SOCIAL DEVIANCE SCALE

1. I found it hard to be objective about parents who were drug addicts.
2. Hostility in the clients was very disturbing.
3. I found it hard to be objective about parents who beat their children.

Responses on these items leaned toward the high scores, indicating a trend toward disagreement with these statements and therefore to profess ability to tolerate deviance. Those with low scores expressed mixed feelings or greater uncertainty about what they felt in this area.

Role Deprivation

To measure the concept of role deprivation, an index based on six questionnaire statements was used. Workers were asked to indicate the extent to which the following statements characterized their agencies.

1. The size of the case load made it difficult to do any real casework.
2. Workers were given plenty of time to work out the best plans for the child.
3. It was easier to withstand pressure from the clients than from the agency.
4. The agency was excessively concerned with the number of cases closed.
5. The agency valued workers who took the initiative and used their imagination.
6. The agency valued mainly the workers who responded to supervision.

The workers' response was fairly well-distributed on a range from those who agreed with the first, third, fourth statements and disagreed with the others (the "deprived") and those who responded with the reverse pattern, indicating that they did not feel deprived.

Administrative Support

The comments of some workers in the main study suggested that they saw the administration as the "enemy," as in the case of one worker who said that "workers and supervisors are sabotaged by the people above them."

Other workers thought that administration was making genuine efforts "to make things workable." From such statements, it was hypothesized that workers who perceived the hierarchy as supportive would have a more favorable outcome than those who did not. To measure this concept, an index was developed which was composed of two interview statements and six responses to questionnaire itmes, on which the high scorers were those who perceived the administration as supportive. As the description of the sample suggested, scores tended toward the lower end of the range, suggesting a trend toward the perception of the administration as nonsupportive. Nevertheless, the range was broad enough to distinguish between those whose views of the administration were relatively positve and those whose were strongly negative.

1. Respondent's attitude toward agency hierarchy.
2. Respondent's acceptance of agency values.
3. It was easier to withstand pressure from the clients than the agency.
4. The agency was excessively concerned with the number of cases closed.
5. If quick action on a case was needed, it was easy to get higher level officials.
6. The agency valued workers who took the initiative or used their imagination.
7. The agency valued mainly the workers who responded well to supervision.
8. Higher level of officials could give useful suggestions on the handling of difficult cases.

Value of the Work
Material from the main study indicated that many of the workers might well have been able to tolerate the pressures of their work had they been able to maintain a belief in the value of their work either for their clients as a group or for society as a whole. It was hypothesized that the greater the worker's confidence in the ultimate value of the services rendered, the greater the likelihood of a favorable outcome—either in the form of advanced training or in job stability.

This hypothesis was measured by an index involving five related assessments made by the workers during the interview with respect to the following:

1. The quality of agency service.
2. The extent to which children's failure to benefit was due to staff inadequacies.
3. Whether parents' failure to benefit was due to staff inadequacies.
4. Whether children's failure to benefit was due to staff inadequacies.
5. The adequacy of the child welfare system in general.

Again respondents could be ranged from low scorers with a low level of conviction about the value of their work to high scorers who were at least relatively comfortable in this respect.

The extent to which the attitudes reflected in these measures influenced workers' interest in professional training and their stability in their jobs and affected their work with their clients will be discussed in Chapter 9. The extent to which public and voluntary agency workers differed on these and other measures will be discussed in chapter 10.

Summary

The aim of this substudy of child welfare workers was to assess the impact of their work experience on their career decisions. Data were collected on a sample of 222 workers approximately three years after they were interviewed for the main study. During this interval, 34 percent had made no changes in their academic status as BA's, 33 percent had partial training, and 21 percent had received MSWs. The remaining 12 percent were oriented to other fields. With respect to employment, 64 percent were continuing with the same agencies (but most of these had transferred to other departments or were holding different positions), 16 percent were working for other agencies (usually in fields other than child welfare), while 20 percent had left social work for unrelated occupations or to remain at home.

Most had made the decision to enter social work after having been interested in other careers or having tried other fields of employment. Many had been hampered by a less than positive image of social workers. The personal influence of friends or relatives in the field played a strong role in their choice of social work. Most were looking for or attracted by the possibility of working with people. Most felt relatively uncommitted to the social work field but became more committed in the course of their experience. The sense of commitment developed despite the high level of discomfort with working conditions, training perceived as inadequate, a low professional level of agency staff, services perceived as inadequate, high tension in the agency atmosphere, inadequate consultation, and resentment of the agency hierarchy.

Most respondents were closely supervised but experienced some turnover among supervisors within a relatively short time period. Nevertheless most evaluations of supervisory relations were positive. Most workers had case loads composed of clients of different ethnic and class origins but the majority denied being troubled by ethnic or class differences or felt they had resolved and handled them adequately. Most workers considered both the quality and quantity of services given by their agencies as poor but acknowledged at least some benefits to some children. Most were equally critical of the system as a whole and considered it in need of major change.

Many of the variables on which respondents expressed different points of view on various aspects of their work were combined to form indices. These included their tendency to accept or reject authority, their tolerance for ambiguity, their perception of the need for change, their orientation to clients or agency procedures, and their assessments of the adequacy of their training. The indices also reflected the workers' ability to tolerate deviance among their clients, their feelings of role deprivation, of administrative support, and of the value of their work.

chapter nine

FINDINGS:
PROFESSIONALIZATION,
MOBILITY,
AND IMPACT ON CLIENTS

A NALYSIS OF THE DATA DESCRIBED in the previous chapter yielded a variety of findings. Some of the hyptheses formulated were upheld, others were not, and some relationships proved to be significant in the opposite direction from what was expected. The analysis also differed in a number of ways from what was originally anticipated. When the substudy of child welfare workers was planned, it was thought that the outcome variable would be a continuum combining both the factors of stability and professional training. On it the workers were placed in a range from the least desirable status (in which the worker was not trained and did not remain in the field), to the theoretically most desirable (in which she received her MSW and remained in her job). As was indicated in chapter 8, such a breakdown would have involved at least seven different categories or points on the continuum.

When the data were ready for computer processing, this ideal definition of outcome had to be discarded for a number of reasons. The fact that the sample size was smaller than anticipated meant that several categories had too few cases for a viable analysis. More important, a preliminary analysis indicated that variables which were significantly related to training were not necessarily influential when related to job stability, and vice versa. Only six variables proved to be significantly related to both outcomes. The outcome variables were somewhat related, but only in one direction: those who leave the field are more likely to be untrained but those who remain do not necessarily obtain a professional degree. It became clear that factors which influenced workers' decisions to train were not the same as those which influenced them to change jobs; therefore a separate analysis of each was warranted.

Analytic problems related to mobility also proved to be more complex than those related to training. Fully 81 percent of the respondents had made some change in their employment status. Those who had changed status could be located on a continuum of distance from the original position which, as was seen in Table 8.1, ranged over six categories: those who were on educational or maternity leave but were committed to return to the agency, those who continued with the same agency but in a different department or in a different position, those who changed to jobs in other child welfare agencies, those in social work positions in other fields, those in non–social work occupations, and those not employed.

The analysis was also complicated by a strong difference between the type of mobility characterizing public agencies and that characterizing voluntary agency workers. Among the public agency respondents, 78 percent remained with their employer, while in voluntary agencies only 39 percent did. The data also indicated that public agency workers moved around much more within the system than did voluntary agency workers. The difference between these two samples will be discussed in detail in chapter 10.

Still another complicating factor in the analysis was the presence of 26 workers whose careers were directed toward fields other than social work, which particularly affected the findings related to professional training. For this reason, these findings will focus on 196 workers whose career interests were either clearly directed toward social work or who were continuing in social work positions without other career interests. The data on those workers who were aiming for other careers will be presented separately. These findings will be followed by those related to occupational mobility.

Most important, it was possible to relate the findings on the worker characteristics identified in the substudy to the actions and attitudes they expressed toward the clients they had served in the main study sample. Relationships were found between a number of worker characteristics and the discharge rate, the perception of improvement in the children and their families, frequency of contact, and optimism about their potential for returning home. The findings in relation to training and mobility will be summarized, since they have been reported elsewhere. The main focus of the chapter will be on the findings related to the impact on clients.

Professionalization

In general, the findings about the achievement of professional training indicated that the strongest correlates were a cluster of interrelated attitudes, the strongest of which is an unwillingness to accept authority. This trait was associated with a strong client orientation, strong convictions about the need for social change, and dissatisfaction with the in-service training given by the agency. Other influential factors were resentment of the status accorded to the fully trained MSW's and the psychiatric consultants and the development of a specialized identification with either the child or the parent client. A relatively early choice of social work as a career and a decision to remain single also contribute to the completion of training.

Personality Measures
Both of the personality measures described in chapter 8 proved to be significant when related to training. The proportion of respondents whose scores indicated a tendency to reject authority (66 percent) was markedly higher for those who had begun or completed training than for those who remained untrained (34 percent). Also, the higher the tolerance for ambiguity, the greater the likelihood that the respondent had completed training.

Need for Change
When the "Need for Change" scale was related to professional training, the results indicated that respondents with scores on the moderate or "liberal" end of the scale were significantly more likely to have started or completed training (56 percent) than those who were more conservative (36 percent).

Client-Procedure Orientation
The hypothesis that the client-oriented would be likely to seek training while the procedure-oriented would more often be content to remain un-

trained was upheld by the findings—58 percent of the client-oriented were trained, in contrast to 31 percent of the procedure-oriented.

Adequacy of Training

The hypothesis that satisfaction with in-service training would motivate workers to enter into full professional training was not upheld. In fact, the relationship proved to be the reverse of what was expected: workers who saw their initial training as inadequate were the ones most likely to have completed work for an MSW.

This finding, however, raises the problem of circularity. Since data on both variables were obtained at the same time, it is equally possible that workers were retrospectively evaluating their initial training as inadequate from the perspective of those who had had a more complete education.[1] This does not negate the possibility that dissatisfaction with their training provided some impetus for their plans to enter school. It is worth noting that partially trained workers were just as likely to describe their training as adequate as were those who had not been exposed to graduate training at all. From this, one may infer that positive opinions about the agency's training program may diminish the desire or the need to complete formal training.

"Anti-elitism"

Another influence on training which proved to be the reverse of what was expected was that of "anti-elitism." It was hypothesized that resentment of the professional elite would act as a push out of the field, since the experienced but not formally trained worker might feel she lacked recognition. The analysis indicated the reverse effect: those who expressed such resentment were more likely to have undertaken or completed training than those who did not.

Timing of Career Decision

Another factor associated with entry into training was the timing of the decision. Of the extensive data obtained in the respondent's accounts of their work histories, only the timing of the decision was significantly related to entry into formal training. The earlier the interest in social work developed and the earlier the decision to aim for graduate training,

1. For this observation, I am indebted to Dr. Trudy Festinger of the New York University Graduate School of Social Work.

the greater the likelihood that partial or full training had been achieved, upholding the hypotheses formulated.

Identification with Parent or Child Clients

Another factor which proved unexpectedly to be related to the completion of graduate social work training was the extent to which workers developed a specialized identification, either with child clients or their parents.

Interviewers were asked to make a judgment as to the extent to which the respondents, in discussing their case loads, appeared to be particularly identified with either children or parents. The majority (75 percent) were perceived as equally identified with both or did not show any inclination to identify with one or the other. Fifteen percent were judged to be identifying primarily with children and ten percent with parents. It seemed likely that the development of more specialized interests would act as a pull toward training. This hypothesis was upheld: the findings indicated that the small group of respondents who had developed either pattern of identification were more likely to be trained than those whose interests appeared less specialized.

Unresponsiveness of Clients

Of the data obtained in relation to the respondents' case loads, only one variable showed a significant relationship with training. As was indicated in chapter 8, respondents were asked to name client traits which were sources of satisfaction or dissatisfaction in their work. In discussing their dissatisfactions, the problem most commonly mentioned was the client's apparent lack of desire to establish a relationship with the worker. Clients were seen as hostile, withdrawn, or unable to acknowledge their problems. This relationship just missed statistical significance at the .05 level in cross-tabulation but accounted for a statistically significant degree of variance in the regression analysis. The analysis indicated that the minority—those who did not find client relationships a major frustration—were more likely to have begun or completed training.

Marital Status

Of the demographic variables examined in the study, the only one which emerged as influential in relation to training was that of marital status when combined with sex.

The findings indicated that when single males were compared to married males, those who were single were more likely to have attained partial or full training. When single females were compared to married females, the singles were also more likely to be trained; but the difference is much less sharp. Thus it appeared that the difference between the demands marriage usually makes on men and those it makes on women were more related to the completion of training than was the sex difference itself. Being male may be a powerful deterrent to entering the field to begin with, but being married is a deterrent to full professionalization once a man is in the field.

Workers with Other Career Interests
As was indicated earlier, 26 workers (or 10 percent of the total sample) either were or had been using their employment in social work as a temporary source of support while they prepared for careers in other fields. Since most of these careers were in service professions (teaching, school guidance, clinical psychology, etc.), some or most of these people might conceivably have been recruited to social work had they found their employment attractive enough.

Since the number of individuals involved is small, neither detailed analysis nor definitive conclusions are feasible, but some comparisons with the majority of workers who were directed toward social work is instructive. Those directed to other careers were a younger group: half of them were under 28—in contrast to one-third of those who had no plans for training or who were partially or fully trained. More striking was that on a number of key measures, they outdid the social workers. Three-fourths of those directed to other careers had scores which indicated a strong rejection of authority, while only a little over half of those embarked on social work careers had such scores. Sixty percent had a strong client orientation in contrast to 43 percent of those in social work training, while three-quarters had high (liberal) scores on the scale measuring need for social change in contrast to two-thirds of those trained in social work.

Early negative images of social workers were significantly more frequently reported by those workers who were aiming for other careers (40 percent) than those who had no plans for any kind of graduate training (19 percent) and those who had partial or full social work training (25 percent). Thus, although the respondents pursuing other careers had had work experience that might have modified their original images somewhat, the experience apparently had not been sufficiently positive to offset the impact of these earlier stereotypes. The evident result was the loss to the field of a group with characteristics compatible with the demands of the profession.

Mobility

The most effective way of analyzing the complex picture of mobility in the study sample involved distinguishing different types of mobility, comparing each in turn to the rest of the sample. These were the internally mobile (those who moved within the agency system), and the professionally mobile (those who left the agency). Of the latter group, those who moved into other social work positions could be distinguished from those who left the field either for non–social work employment or to remain at home. Variables related to each form of mobility were usually, but not always, different.

Internal Mobility

What distinguished those who moved within the agency system from the others? The findings indicated that this group, apparently more than any other, was influenced by friends employed in the field. In recounting their occupational histories, respondents were asked with whom they had discussed their decision to enter the field and how they had been influenced; 26 percent of the sample named friends already employed in social work, the largest group of referents mentioned. The analysis indicated that the respondents who were so influenced were more likely to have made internal changes: only 13 percent of the stable group mentioned such an influence in contrast to 33 percent of those who made changes within the agency.

It is possible that the "influential" friends in social work who contributed to the initial decision may also have been sources of information as to where transfer within the system was possible. Whatever the explanation, this was the only form of mobility in which variables of this kind showed any influence. Nor was there any other variable showing a significant influence on internal mobility when the factor of agency auspices was controlled. This is probably related to the fact that many of the transfers, as noted earlier, resulted from higher level administrative decisions and not from individual motivations.

Agency mobility

What distinguished those who left their agencies from those who stayed, whether they remained in their original positions or transferred to another department? Three variables emerged as important in relation to this form of mobility, the most significant of which was the extent to which the respondent was client-oriented. Of those who were strongly client-oriented, 47 percent remained with the agency in contrast to 68 percent of those with a procedure orientation or a mixture of the two.

Age and ethnicity were also factors in agency mobility. As would be expected, the youngest group of workers, those under twenty-eight, tended to leave the agency in decidedly greater numbers than did their elders. Of those under twenty-eight, 49 percent had left the agency in contrast to 29 percent of those between twenty-eight and thirty-one and 27 percent of those over twenty-one. With respect to ethnicity, the non-white minority, representing 22 percent of the sample, were more likely to remain with the agency than the white majority: 80 percent as compared to 60 percent. Age, however, interacted with client-orientation (the client-oriented tended to be younger than the procedure-oriented) and also interacted with ethnicity (white workers tended to be younger than non-white). The regression analysis indicated that client-orientation accounted for more variance in agency mobility than either age or ethnicity. Furthermore, the expectation that workers who developed neither a client- nor a procedure-orientation would leave the profession was not upheld. Those with a "mixed" orientation tended to behave like the procedure-oriented and remain with the agency.

Professional Mobility

What distinguished those who found other positions in social work from the rest of the sample? Those who made this change were more likely to be single, to have mentioned client-hostility as a problem in cross-class and -cultural relations, and were also more likely to be client-oriented.

Data on marital status indicated that both the married and the single respondents had left their original employer in almost equal proportions: 63 percent for the singles, and 66 percent for the married. The dif-

ference, of course, lay in what they did when they left. The single respondent took another position; the married one was the more likely to
remain at home.

As the previous chapter indicated, 41 percent of the respondents who
were aware of class and cultural differences referred to differences in
middle and lower-class lifestyles; 32 percent mentioned language problems, while 24 percent mentioned hostility on social or class grounds. Of
those who were aware of client hostility, 38 percent had changed positions within the profession in contrast to 19 percent of those for whom it
was not a problem.

As was indicated earlier, a client orientation was an influential factor
in leaving the agency, but the analysis also indicated that the client-
oriented were more likely to remain in the field in other social work positions than to leave it altogether. Twenty-six percent of the client-oriented
were in other social work positions as compared to 13 percent of the
procedure-oriented. The latter, if they left the agency at all, were more
likely to leave the field as well.

Occupational Mobility

What distinguished those who left the field, either for non–social work
employment or to remain at home? As was indicated earlier, to be married was an obvious contributing factor.

Ethnicity also emerged as an important variable in relation to occupational mobility. Not only were the non-white workers significantly more
likely to remain in the same agency than the white workers, but they
were also much less likely to defect from the profession. Eight percent of
the non-white workers left the field, in contrast to 24 percent of the
whites. It seems likely that white workers see a broader range of occupational choices for themselves and feel freer to change than do non-whites.

The analysis indicated, however, that an even stronger factor in defec-
tion was the presence of the negative image of social work, referred to
earlier. Of those who had such images, 33 percent were no longer in
social work, about twice the proportion of those whose images were more
neutral or positive. These were largely respondents who apparently had
other career plans from the beginning and were using social work jobs as
a means of supporting themselves while getting degrees in other fields.

Even more significant than the negative image was dissatisfaction with
the responsiveness of clients. As was indicated earlier, the most com-

monly mentioned form of dissatisfaction was the client's lack of desire to establish a relationship with the worker. The absence of this complaint distinguished the occupationally stable from all others: 49 percent of the stable mentioned this problem in contrast to 66 percent of all those who were mobile. In contrasting the defectors to all those who were mobile within the profession, it was found that 86 percent mentioned this lack of client response, in contrast to 68 percent of the professionally mobile. In other words, all mobile respondents reported this form of dissatisfaction more frequently than those who were stable, but the defectors were even more likely to report it.

Impact on Clients

Having examined the impact of the workers' experience on their careers, we can proceed to examine the links between the two studies. The findings reported in chapter 7 indicated that the worker's assessment of the mother was the most powerful variable among all of those studied as influencing the discharge rate. The data in the substudy raise such related questions as the following: Is the client-oriented worker more likely to discharge the children in her care? Is she more or less likely to perceive improvement? What impact, if any, does the worker's discouragement or frustration about the nature of her work in general have on the status of the families she works with?

In the main study, the measures that reflected pressure on workers or discomfort in their work showed no significant relationship with any of the three outcome variables. Those data, however, were obtained at the end of a lengthy interview focused on the study subject and were necessarily brief and relatively superficial. The data on worker attitudes in the substudy were obtained in greater depth under more favorable conditions and can therefore be assumed to contain more valid reflections of the workers' feelings. The obvious disadvantage is that the sample from which these data were obtained was smaller and less representative than the main study sample. Furthermore, questions can be raised about the appropriateness of relating data on worker attitudes to actions taken in relation to families and children three years earlier. The analysis suggested that such attitudes as those reflected in the measure called "client-orientation," associated as it was with an early decision to embark on a career in social work, are stable and could be seen as bearing some relation to worker feelings at the time the children and families in question were being served. Workers may have been more or less client-oriented in 1966 than they perceived themselves to be when they were interviewed in 1970, but it seems unlikely that a worker who was strongly client-oriented in 1970 was procedure-oriented in 1966 or vice versa. The time gap has the added value of assuring that the two classes of data are independent of each other.

As will be seen later, when the findings are presented in detail, the direction of the relationship between the main study and the substudy data is not always the same. In most instances, it is logical to assume that the data obtained in the substudy preceded or existed concurrently with the main study data. In other instances, it is more plausible to assume that the main study data represent the initial condition and the attitudes described by the substudy are a consequence. In some instances, plausible explanations are possible in either direction and both seem equally valid.

Each worker in the ancillary study was matched with one family served in the main study. Since most workers at Time 1 had reported on more than one family, it was necessary to make a choice, often among several families. The family chosen was the one whom the worker had known closest to eight months, the modal time period covered by the Time 1 interview. It was assumed that controlling for time would also control other variables such as the frequency of contact and knowledge of the family. In cases where the worker had reported on several families during the same time period, one of these was chosen at random. Analysis followed the same pattern used in both the main study and the substudy. Worker attitudes described in the substudy were cross-tabulated against the three forms of outcomes used in the main study: discharge, improvement in the family, and improvement in the child. Several main-study variables, such as the frequency of contact between workers and clients or the workers' optimism about discharge, were also significantly related to some of the data in the substudy. A regression analysis was also done to determine the extent to which the variables from the substudy were interrelated and to assess their relative influence on the main study data.

Discharge

At Time 1, children were more likely to be discharged from public shelters or from other temporary facilities than from long-term voluntary agencies. Therefore, some of the substudy variables related to discharge reflect conditions prevalent in the public agency. Workers who thought they were poorly informed about the nature of their work, who reported a high incidence of emergencies, and who saw a great need for change in the child welfare system all tended to discharge children in their care significantly more frequently than the better informed—those who dealt with fewer emergencies, and saw less need for change. All those variables, as will be seen in the next chapter, were strongly associated with employment in the public agency.

Other variables, however, showed an influence on discharge which was significant even when the factor of agency auspices was controlled. As was reported in chapter 8, when asked to name the major frustration of child welfare work, half the workers mentioned lack of services and facilities, a form of frustration mentioned much more frequently than any of the others. The proportion of discharges made was more than twice as high for those workers who mentioned lack of services than for those who did not, as Table 9.1 indicates. The second most frequently mentioned frustration—a sense of helplessness—is also related to a disproportionately high discharge rate but the relationship is not so strong as with lack of services.

TABLE 9.1

Frustration Over Lack of Services and Discharge at Time 1
(N = 216) [a]

Status	Lack of Services Mentioned (N = 110) %	Not Mentioned (N = 106) %
Discharged	30	13
Remained in care	70	87
	100	100

[a] Chi-square = 7.982; significant at .005 with 1 df.

As was noted in chapter 8, workers were questioned about the extent to which they used informal procedures in service to clients, as part of an attempt to assess the extent to which they adhered literally to regulations or managed to find ways to cut the red tape. A minority of the respondents seemed to have little or no understanding of what was meant by such procedures and obviously did not use them. This group was significantly less likely than the majority to discharge the children in their care, as Table 9.2 indicates.

TABLE 9.2

Informal Procedures and Discharge (N = 217)

	Used (N = 164) %	Not Used (N = 53) %
Status		
Discharged	25	9
Remained in care	75	91
	100	100

[a] Chi-square = 4.916; significant at .027 with 1 df.

Family Improvement

No strong pattern emerged from the analysis of perception of improvement in the family. A few statistically significant differences were seen but were difficult to explain and may have been the result of chance.

Child Improvement

Client-oriented workers were significantly more likely to perceive improvement in children than were those with a mixed orientation and were much more likely to see improvement than the procedure-oriented.

TABLE 9.3

Client Orientation and the Perception of Improvement in Children [a]
(N = 155) [b]

	Client-Oriented (N = 55) %	Mixed (N = 66) %	Procedure-Oriented (N = 34) %
Status			
Child unimproved	40	56	79
Improved	60	44	21
	100	100	100

[a] This analysis included only those workers who worked directly with children.
[b] Chi-square = 13.222; significant at .002 with 2 df.

Contact with the Mother

Additional analysis of the substudy in relation to the main study involved treating some of the variables, used as independent variables in the latter study, as dependent variables. In other words, having established that frequency of contact with the family was associated with a higher discharge rate, one could look for factors associated with the workers' investment of time. The analysis indicated a strong relationship between some of the more negative attitudes expressed about the system and the frequency of contact. The more radical workers were in their opinions of the child welfare system, the more they thought it required extensive change, and the more likely they were to have had relatively high degree of contact with the mothers they were seeing.

TABLE 9.4

Need for Change in the Child Welfare System and Contact with the Mother (N = 163) [a]

	Little or No Change (N = 79)	Extensive Change (N = 84)
Contact	%	%
Limited [b]	69	40
Three or more interviews	31	60
	100	100

[a] Chi-square = 12.282; significance under .001 with 1 df.
[b] Defined as two interviews or less during the eight month period covered by the Time 1 interview.

This is another finding that also can be interpreted in the reverse direction. It is possible that more extensive contact with clients led to greater knowledge of their problems and reinforced the workers' perception of the need for change. Probably the attitude and the associated activity reinforced each other. Those who were more critical of the system wanted to see children discharged and worked harder with the families to see to it that discharge took place.

Two other variables showed the same pattern of relationship between negative attitudes and extensive contact. The more skeptical they were about the parents' ability to benefit from help, the more likely they were to have been in contact with parents more frequently than was typical for

TABLE 9.5

Contact with Parents and Belief that They Benefit (N = 159) [a]

	Parents Do Not Benefit (N = 87)	Parents Benefit (N = 72)
Contact	%	%
Average or less	54	71
Above average	46	29
	100	100

[a] Chi-square = 4.024; significant at .045 with 1 df.

workers during the first year of placement. Again, the reverse relationship is also plausible: the more contact they had, the more skeptical workers became about the potential for parents to benefit.

Another factor related to the degree of contact with the family was the workers' report of the agency atmosphere. Unlike the preceding variables, agency "atmosphere" had to precede or be concurrent with the workers' activity and did not lend itself to circular interpretation. As Table 9.6 indicates, the greater the tension reported by the worker, the greater the contact with the mother.

TABLE 9.6

Contact with Mother and Agency Atmosphere (N = 166) [a]

Contact	Relatively Tense Atmosphere (N = 106) %	Relatively Positive Atmosphere (N = 60) %
Limited	47	65
Three or more interviews	53	35
	100	100

[a] Chi-square = 4.207; significant at .041 with 1 df.

As was noted in chapter 8, the workers reported that field travel was unobjectionable because, among other things, it could provide an escape from office tensions. Thus the more tension, the greater the need to "escape" by visiting families. It is also likely that both factors were associated with more active workers: the worker who was more perceptive or sensitive to agency atmosphere was also the one more likely to be active with clients.

Not surprisingly, the "client-oriented" had significantly more contact with mothers than those with mixed or "procedure" orientations.

TABLE 9.7

Client-Orientation and Contact with Mother (N = 169) [a]

Contact	Client-Oriented (N = 69) %	Mixed- or Procedure-Oriented (N = 100) %
Limited	45	60
Three or more interviews	55	40
	100	100

[a] Chi-square = 5.299; significant at .05 with 1 df.

Contact with Children

The degree of contact workers had with children was also related to a number of variables derived from the substudy, in some instances the same and in others different from those related to contact with the family. Workers who doubted that the parents benefited from the system were also more likely to have had a greater degree of contact with children than those who believed that parents did benefit.

TABLE 9.8

Contact with Children and Belief that Parents Benefit
(N = 154) [a]

	Parents Do Not Benefit (N = 83)	Parents Benefit (N = 71)
Contact	%	%
Average contact	60	78
Above average	40	22
	100	100

[a] Chi-square = 4.469; significant at .035 with 1 df.

Workers who made their career decisions early—while still in college—tended to have an above-average degree of contact with children— 44 percent in contrast to 28 percent for those who made their career decisions later.

Three worker attitudes showed relationships with the degree of contact with children which just missed statistical significance at the .05 level but accounted for significant degrees of variance in the regression analysis. Thirty-eight percent of the workers who complained about lack of responsiveness on the part of clients had above-average contact with children in contrast to 22 percent of those who did not express such a concern; 39 percent of the workers with a high tolerance for client deviance had above average contact with children in contrast to 24 percent of those with low tolerance; 41 percent of the workers with an "anti-placement" bias had above-average contact with children in contrast to 23 percent of those who were "pro-placement" on this measure.

Optimism about Length of Care

As was indicated in chapter 4, workers in the main study were asked to predict how long the child was likely to remain in care. As Table 9.9 illustrates, those workers in the substudy who scored high on the index measuring their perception of the need for change were much more likely than their more conservative colleagues to predict that the child would return home and would not remain in care for the duration of his childhood.

TABLE 9.9

Need for Change and Optimism About Discharge (N = 174) [a]

	Conservative to Moderate (N = 135)	Radical (N = 39)
Prediction	%	%
Permanent foster care	51	28
Discharge	49	72
	100	100

[a] Chi-square = 5.503; significant at .02 with 1 df.

On the face of it, this would seem to be an unusually optimistic prediction for the more radical workers, but it may also have been an expression of a wish that the children with whom they are identified would "escape" the system rather than a realistic assessment of the child's future.

On the other hand, workers who scored high on the measure reflecting feelings of administrative support were also more likely to predict that children would eventually go home than those who perceived that the administration was unsupportive or only occasionally supportive. This relationship just misses statistical significance in a 2 × 2 table but accounts by itself for 2 percent of the variance in the regression analysis.

TABLE 9.10

Administrative Support and Optimism about Discharge (N = 173) [a]

	Relatively Unsupportive (N = 112)	Supportive (N = 61)
Prediction	%	%
Permanent foster care	52	36
Discharge	48	64
	100	100

[a] Chi-square = 3.319; significant at .06 with 1 df.

Since the "radical" workers were not the ones who perceived the administration as supportive, it seems evident that optimism about discharge could stem from different sources with different workers. The more conservative, pro-administration workers may have felt that the system works as it should—that is, toward reuniting families—and may have been relatively optimistic about the likelihood that the child would return home. Whatever the direction of worker assessments about the prognosis for children in their care, the predictions were apparently influenced by their assessments of the specific agency or of the system as a whole.

Summary of Findings

Entry into full professional training was associated with a tendency to reject authority, a capacity to tolerate ambiguity, strong convictions about the need for social change, a strong orientation toward service to clients, and dissatisfaction with agency training. Other factors also related to entry into formal traning were resentment of the "elite" status assigned to trained professionals, the development of an identification with either child or parent clients, and lack of feelings that clients were unresponsive to workers. Relatively early decisions to enter social work (i.e., before the completion of college) and avoidance of marriage, especially among men, contributed to the completion of training.

The analysis of mobility indicated that each form of occupational change—transfer within the agency, changing positions within the profession, and leaving the field—was associated with different influences. Internal mobility differed from the other forms of mobility in that this change was related to the influence of peers, rather than to the pressures of working conditions, personality trends, or social situations reflected in such variables as age, marital status, or ethnicity.

Other forms of mobility involving more drastic decisions to change jobs or leave the field were associated with some form of dissatisfaction with client–worker relations. Factors relating to social status such as age, marriage, ethnicity, and the history of occupational choice affected some forms of mobility but not others. The mobile worker felt either a general lack of response from clients or a more specific form of hostility on racial or class grounds; otherwise she had an orientation toward clients in which the need to give service was apparently not met by the job.

As was indicated in chapter 8, workers left or transferred because of family-connected problems, a desire to enter school, or for agency-related problems such as reorganization, dissatisfaction with the salary, or lack of opportunity for advancement. There was not a single instance of a change consciously made because of dissatisfaction with client relations, even as a secondary factor. Apparently the link between the strain in client–worker relationships and changing jobs was not consciously perceived by the worker or could not be expressed directly, because it was too unacceptable. It may be too great a threat to professional self-esteem to admit that difficulty in establishing relationships could be so pervasive as to be a factor in changing jobs. Feelings that one may be deserting the clients most in need also may be too unacceptable for open expression.

When matched with the clients served in the main study, a number of the variables described in the substudy were found to be significantly related to the discharge of children from care. Factors associated with public agency workers who were responsible for most of the early discharges—coping with frequent emergencies, feelings of being poorly informed, perception of a need for major changes in the system—were all related to a comparatively high discharge rate. Independently of public-agency employment, workers' feelings of frustration about the adequacy of service were also related to a high discharge rate, as was their ability to use informal procedures.

Client-oriented workers were more likely to perceive improvement in children than were the procedure-oriented.

Relatively frequent contact with families was associated with the perception of need for change in the system, skepticism about the parents' ability to benefit from help, perception of tensions in the agency atmosphere, and a client-orientation. Relatively frequent contact with children was also associated with skepticism about the parents' ability to benefit from help. So also was an early decision to enter social work, complaints about the lack of responsiveness in clients, a high tolerance for client deviance, and an "anti-placement" bias.

Optimism about the length of time children would remain in care was associated with the perception of a strong need for change, as was the perception that the administration was supportive.

In reviewing these findings, it is worth noting that two measures of worker attitudes toward clients—perception of the client's lack of desire for relationships and the "client-orientation"—are significantly related to each of the forms of outcome examined: they affected the decision to undertake training, the decision to change jobs, and had some impact on the perception of improvement in children.

It is also noteworthy that some variables which affected career decisions were unrelated to client actions, and vice versa. Personal factors, such as age, sex, marital status, personality traits, and other career interests were relevant for career decisions but had little impact on clients. Three work-related variables—identification with parent or child clients, resentment of trained professionals, and the perception of in-service training as inadequate—were also related to career decisions, but had no perceptible impact on client-related behavior.

On the other hand, some work-related conditions and attitudes—skepticism about the value of one's work, use of informal methods, a sense of administrative support—played no apparent role in career decisions, but had significance for client-related behavior.

Some negative findings are also worth noting, since they refer to common-sense assumptions about occupational mobility, to factors usually considered important in the profession, or to expectations raised from the findings of other studies.

Since complaints about physical discomforts were widespread, they might have been expected to have some influence on the worker's decision to leave—either to enter school or make some sort of occupational change or else have some effect on client-related behavior. Apart from the fact that the frequency of emergencies affected the discharge rate, working conditions showed no demonstrable relationship to the problems considered here. Neither did actual differences in salary nor the perception of relative deprivation when compared to friends' earnings.

Another group of variables which proved to be less important than was expected—considering the significance frequently attached to them by practitioners—are those related to supervision. Although workers, as noted, usually evaluated their supervisors in favorable terms and were usually closely supervised, there was no indication that this or any other aspect of supervision influenced either the worker's decision to enter graduate school or to change jobs, nor did supervision seem to have any direct influence on the variables used to measure client impact. Thus there was no indication that supervisors serve as role models for beginning workers. It is possible that, given the turnover most workers experienced, few supervisory relationships, however positive they may have been reported to be, were strong enough to have had such an impact.

It is also worth noting that peer relations as expressed through informal interaction with fellow workers showed no apparent effect on any of the forms of outcome examined, despite the fact that many workers stressed the importance of such relations in their work.

Discussion

It is important to note that the selection processes suggested by the findings are both functional and dysfunctional for the profession. On the one hand, it is encouraging to see that much of the "selection" is in the right direction: people who are client-oriented, see the need for social change, can tolerate ambiguity, can develop an identification or interest in a particular client group, and do not see their clients as unresponsive would be seen by most of those in the field as highly suited to it. Whether the "rejection of authority" is a favorable form of selection depends on one's point of view. Insofar as this pattern implies that workers who complete training are more apt to be independent, it may be seen as a favorable selective force.

On the other hand, one may wonder how functional it is for the child welfare field that workers may be using graduate school as an escape from authority; they may be reacting to the inadequacies of in-service training and be resentful of the status or the prestige accorded the fully trained.

It should also be kept in mind that most of the untrained continue in the field. If the graduate school of social work in effect draws away the client-oriented, those who are most open to change, and those who tolerate ambiguity, then by implication, the agencies are overstaffed by those with the opposing characteristics: the "procedure-oriented," the conservatives, those who cannot tolerate ambiguity—i.e., the "bureaucratics." Agencies would need the budgetary resources and an active interest in attracting the "client-oriented" to return in order to offset this trend. Without this, the selection process only reinforces the status quo—i.e., the long-standing schism between the overburdened large agencies (usually public, but not always) and the smaller, more specialized agencies who maintain high professional standards.

Discussions of social-work manpower problems usually place heavy stress on the problems of attracting people to the field, as though numerical expansion would solve most, if not all, of its problems. The findings here suggest that there is at least as much, if not more, need to understand what is happening in the field under current conditions, in which the profession recruits personnel by employing them first and selectively training them later.

The findings about mobility also suggest that emphasis on expansion and more adequate staffing will do little to solve the key problem. It is difficult to see how the recruitment of larger numbers of workers to the field would have any impact on the problem of unsatisfactory client–worker relations, which proved to be the central factor in three of the four types of mobility examined. Experimentation with changes in function might do more to meet the need of those who are now inclined to mobility and help reduce the the turn to a less dysfunctional level.

The findings about the impact of worker attitudes on clients consistently and ironically imply that what may be dysfunctional for the worker is functional for the client. Worker anger and dissatisfaction with the system leads to or is associated with greater activity with families and children which, in turn, significantly enhances their chances of leaving. The findings again tend to support the contention of many workers that the system works against the discharge of children from care. Unless the worker is actively dissatisfied with the quality of service offered, and is willing or able to go beyond formal regulations, the children in their care are most likely to remain there. Further implications of these findings will be discussed in the final chapter.

chapter ten

AGENCY AUSPICES: A COMPARISON OF WORKERS IN PUBLIC AND IN VOLUNTARY AGENCIES

P RACTICE IDEOLOGY in the field of social work has focused heavily on client–worker relationships and less heavily on the organizational contexts in which these relationships develop. The size and the diversity of both the main study and the substudy made it possible and necessary to examine the influence of a number of organizational factors operating in client–worker relationships in foster care. As was noted in chapter 3, an analysis of the influence of organizational variables was not a simple task, since the major variables tended to be interrelated and were also related to important client characteristics. Public agencies are larger than voluntary agencies and larger agencies tend to be multifunctional. Sectarian affiliation and agency auspices were, as expected, associated with particular ethnic groups and with socioeconomic class. The techniques of regression analysis, however, made it possible to sort out the relative influence of these variables and determine which ones were significantly related to the forms of outcome with which each study was concerned. The variables of agency auspices (public vs. voluntary), type of service (institutional vs. foster home), sectarian affiliation, number of clients served, and structural complexity (single vs. dual or multiple functions) were systematically introduced into the main study analysis. Their influence on each form of outcome and their relationships with client and worker characteristics were examined. Because of the smaller size of the substudy sample, only the influence of agency auspices and the type of service was examined.

In general, none of the organizational variables mentioned proved to be a major influence in relation to the discharge of children from care or the workers' perception of improvement in either the children or the families. Generally the same was true for the substudy. An analysis of professionalization and mobility, controlled for agency auspices, showed little real difference between the workers in public agencies and those in voluntary agencies; motivations for workers to enter training or to change jobs were the same for both. The single major difference was the tendency for public workers to transfer to other departments while the voluntary agency workers left their jobs. Nevertheless, a number of differences emerged from the findings of the first year of the study in areas where comparisons between public and voluntary agency workers could be made, and a number of even more striking differences were also seen in the substudy. These merit reporting and can be related to other findings.

The relationship between public and voluntary agencies has been a subject of controversy in the field for much of its relatively brief history. In recent times, the controversy has evolved to the point where the partisans of each acknowledge the other and agree that coexistence is a desirable, even an essential, state. At the same time, it was also clear from observations made throughout the period of this study that the relationship is not a a comfortable one. Levitt's study describes, in detail, the interdependency, the political pressure, and the power struggle between the partners in this intricate system.[1] At this writing, citizens' groups are taking the entire public-voluntary network to court, charging it with failure to give equal service to its clients.[2] The consequences of the suit could force radical changes in the system, changes the discontent and criticisms of practitioners and policymakers have failed to bring about to date.

The findings here summarize the main points of difference and similarity between the two sectors of this network as seen in both the main

1. Louis Levitt, *The Accountability Gap in Foster Care: Discontinuities in Accountability in the Purchase and Provision of Foster Care Services in New York City* (PhD diss., Graduate School of Public Administration, New York University, 1972).
2. *Wilder, et al. v Sugarman, et al.*, class action suit brought by the New York Civil Liberties Union on behalf of children in the city's shelters.

study and the substudy; they are followed by a discussion of the significance of these differences and their implications for the field.

Main Study Findings

As was observed in earlier chapters, the involvement of the public agency
dominated the first year of the study, was substantially reduced in the second year and, apart from isolated cases, was nearly totally absent in the
last two cycles of data collection. This reflects the way the New York City
foster care network is structured: responsibility for the intake process rests
with the public department and is usually transferred to the voluntary sector when it is established that the child's need is for long-term care. Thus
comparisons between public and voluntary agencies are complicated by
these differences in function. Nevertheless, both sectors are part of the
same network and of the same professional subculture, and thus share to
a large extent the same values and goals. As will be noted later, the substudy showed no significant differences in the characteristics of the workers employed, implying that both draw their personnel from much the
same population in the larger society. Other systematic comparisons were
possible with the substudy data, because the problems to which the study
was addressed and the questions asked were relevant for workers from
both sectors. Data from the main study were less focused on the workers,
but there were a number of variables on which valid comparisons could
be made. These fell into two categories: those which reflected attributes
of the staff and those which described specific aspects of the workers' performance in relation to the children in the study.

Staff Attributes

As was expected, comparisons at Time 1 between public and voluntary
agency workers on size of case load, training, and experience, problems
in placement, and work pressure all favored the voluntary agency.

High case loads were much more characteristic of the public system
than of the voluntary system, particularly in the case of the intake agencies. High case loads were less characteristic of the public child caring
agencies but still tended to be heavier than those of the voluntary system.

Worker experience and training also varied with the auspices of the
agency in the expected direction: the highest proportion of trained and
experienced workers were employed by the voluntary agencies, while the

TABLE 10.1

Agency Auspices and Size of Case Load (N = 471) [a]

Case Load Size	Public Child Caring (N = 44) %	Public Intake (N = 189) %	Voluntary Agencies (N = 238) %
3–20	7	14	28
21–30	43	9	31
31–51	23	18	25
51 and over	27	59	16
	100	100	100

[a] Chi-square = 107.04; significant at .0001 level with 6 df.

untrained and least experienced were disproportionately represented in the public agencies.

In two other respects, differences between the two systems were also in the expected direction. The public system was not only "disadvantaged" with respect to case load size and worker experience, but it also had a more problematic clientele. An analysis of client characteristics indicated that the public system cares for a disproportionate number of children

TABLE 10.2

Agency Auspices and Worker Experience (N = 510) [a,b]

Experience	Public (N = 250) %	Voluntary (N = 261) %
Less than 1 year	30	19
1–2 years	22	13
2–3 years; some training	19	23
MSW or 3 years or more experience	29	45
	100	100

[a] Chi-square = 21.546; significant at .0001 level with 3 df.
[b] One worker interviewed refused to give information about herself.

with intelligence scores below 80. Black mothers represented over half of those served by the public system but little over a quarter of those served by the voluntary agencies. Mothers in the lowest socioeconomic category constituted 33 percent of the public agency's clients but only 15 percent of the voluntary agency's. The mothers with the most chronic problems—the alcoholics, drug addicts, and the mentally retarded—were more likely to be found in the care of the public agencies while those with less chronic problems stood an even chance of being involved with either sector.

The main study evidence also supported the expectation that the public system was the more "bureaucratic" and its workers more pressured. It was possible to categorize the obstacles to the placement of the study children as "bureaucratic" (procedural problems within or between agencies) or "nonbureaucratic" (problems related to the community, such as shortages of foster homes). The findings indicate that the public agency workers were significantly more likely to report problems in both categories, particularly those categorized as "bureaucratic."

Another measure, called the index of "worker pressure," used five items reflecting the extent to which workers found working conditions uncomfortable. Here too findings were in the expected direction: voluntary agency workers were significantly more likely to work with relative freedom from pressure than were the public agency workers.

TABLE 10.3

Agency Auspices and Placement Problems (N = 616) [a,b]

Type of Problem	Public (N = 175) %	Voluntary (N = 441) %
None	45	64
Bureaucratic	33	22
Nonbureaucratic	22	14
	100	100

[a] Chi-square = 17.354; significant under .001 with 2 df.
[b] For this table, the child sample was used and thus reflects data given by the workers in direct contact with children. When the same anslysis was repeated with the family sample, the findings showed the same pattern.

TABLE 10.4

Pressure on the Worker and Agency Auspices (N = 510) [a]

Pressure	Public (N = 250) %	Voluntary (N = 260) %
Heavy	9	9
Moderately heavy	23	12
Average	39	30
Below average	22	33
Minimal	7	16
	100	100

[a] Chi-square = 24.774; significant at .0001 with 4 df.

Case Performance

Of eleven variables which described worker activity in relation to study children and their families and which permitted comparison between the voluntary and the public sector workers, six showed no significant differences. Of the six measures on which differences were found, five favored the public agencies while only one favored the voluntary network.

On the index of family contact described in chapter 5, public agency workers were significantly more likely to have scores in the "high frequency" category than voluntary agency workers. Since this might have been attributed to the fact that the public sector has a higher incidence of cases where the children had already been discharged, thus requiring greater contact with families, comparisons were made which controlled for the status of the child. For 143 children still in temporary care, voluntary agencies had a disproportionate number in which contact centered on the families was minimal. The public agencies had a much higher proportion of "average" (once a month) contacts, while families in which activity was high were nearly proportionate in both systems.

When one looks at 90 families whose children had already been discharged, one again finds a higher number of families in the voluntary agency system than in the public system for whom contact is minimal, although here the difference misses statistical significance at the .05 level.

The pattern in both Tables 10.5 and 10.6 is a bimodal one for the voluntary agencies. The families for whom contact was below average and those for whom it was above are disproportionately high, suggesting that some voluntary agencies—or some workers—concentrated heavily on some cases and minimized activity on others.

TABLE 10.5

Frequency of Family-Centered Contact for Children in Interim Care by Agency Auspices (N = 143) [a]

	Public (N = 86)	*Voluntary (N = 57)*
Contact	%	%
Below average	41	56
Average	27	7
Above average	32	37
	100	100

[a] Chi-square = 8.993; significant at .01 with 2 df.

TABLE 10.6

Frequency of Family-Centered Contact Where Children were Discharged by Agency Auspices (N = 90) [a]

Contact	Public (N = 66) %	Voluntary (N = 24) %
Below average	11	29
Average	21	13
Above average	68	58
	100	100

[a] Chi-square = 4.865; significant at .08 with 2 df.

As was indicated in chapter 5, another index was used to measure frequency of contact with children. The analysis indicated that, on this measure, children in public under-care agencies were significantly more likely to receive more attention than those in voluntary under-care agencies.

TABLE 10.7

Frequency of Child-Centered Contact and Agency Auspices (N = 565) [a]

Contact	Public Under-Care (N = 128) %	Voluntary Under-Care (N = 437) %
Minimal	12	17
Below average	15	21
Average	13	23
Above average	30	16
Maximum	30	23
	100	100

[a] Chi-square = 20.506; significant at .0001 with 4 df.

Assuming that it is desirable for agencies at this stage of placement to contact as many members of the extended family as possible, families in care were categorized as (1) those where only the mother was known to the worker, (2) those where only the mother and father were known, (3) those where other members of the family, in addition to one or both parents, had been contacted. The findings indicated that cases in the third category were found almost twice as frequently in the public agency case load as in the voluntary load.

TABLE 10.8

Extent of Family Contact and Agency Auspices (N = 448) [a]

	Public (N = 239)	Voluntary (N = 209)
Family Members	%	%
Mother only	34	47
Both parents	26	32
Parent(s) and others	40	21
	100	100

[a] Chi-square = 20.092; significant at .0001 with 2 df.

It is possible that children in families with actively interested extended families have a greater potential for discharge and are not so likely to be referred to voluntary agencies for long-term care. The public agency is also under more pressure to locate parents and may use relatives to do so. But the fact that so few of the families served by the voluntary sector involve contact with the extended family also suggests that such activity is "written off" in the first year of placement.

Main study data also included a number of measures of worker knowledge. One such was the extent to which workers were able to account for the activities of the agency since the date of placement. The analysis indicated that for 73 percent of the children and 80 percent of the families, workers were able to cover the period of time involved adequately, either through direct knowledge or from the case record. The remainder could account only for events that took place after the case was assigned to them. The high rate of adequate coverage is not surprising in light of the fact that the period covered was typically only eight or nine months. But one would expect that the voluntary agencies, with the advantage of lower case loads and less pressured workers, would have a lower proportion of inadequately reported cases than the public agency. The findings ran counter to this expectation. For the family sample, the public agencies' performance was significantly better. For the child sample, the difference favored the voluntary agencies but missed statistical significance.

Another measure of workers' knowledge was a judgment made by trained coders and based on the worker's ability to answer the interviewers' questions, as well as the amount of detail given. Because of the differences in agency functions, three judgments were necessary: knowledge of the family's history, knowledge of the family's current situation, and knowledge of the child's current situation. The analysis indicated

TABLE 10.9

Adequacy of Coverage and Agency Auspices

	Family Sample (N = 458) [a] %		Child Sample (N = 616) [b] %	
	Public (N = 241)	Voluntary (N = 217)	Public (N = 175)	Voluntary (N = 441)
Coverage	%	%	%	%
Inadequate	14	27	32	25
Adequate	86	73	68	75
	100	100	100	100

[a] Chi-square = 11.279; significant at .001 with 1 df.
[b] Chi-square = 2.820; significant at .08 with 1 df.

that there was no significant difference between public and voluntary agency workers in respect to current knowledge of either the family or the child. Family history was the one measure about which the voluntary agency workers were described as having detailed knowledge more frequently than the public agency workers.

TABLE 10.10

Agency Auspices and Knowledge of Family History
(N = 392) [a,b]

Knowledge	Public (N = 209) %	Voluntary (N = 184) %
Limited	31	23
Moderate	39	29
Detailed	30	48
	100	100

[a] Chi-square = 14.206; significant at .001 with 2 df.
[b] This judgment was not made in cases where knowledge of the family was not required by the worker's function.

Another variable which could be seen as a reflection of the workers' performance was the extent to which workers spontaneously described the unmet needs in the family. In this respect, the public agency workers reported such needs significantly more frequently than did the voluntary agency workers. Since this might have been accounted for by the fact noted earlier that public agency workers served more severely disturbed mothers, this variable was controlled. The difference, however, remained. For 76 mothers suffering from some form of chronic pathology, unmet needs were described more frequently by workers in the public agencies than those in the voluntary agency but the difference missed statistical significance at the .05 level. For the remaining 311 mothers with less extreme disturbances, the perception of unmet needs was also more common in the public sector, a difference which is statistically significant.

TABLE 10.11

Perception of Unmet Needs by Agency Auspices (N = 387)

	Severe Disturbances in Mother (N = 76) [a]		Less Severe Disturbances in Mother (N = 311) [b]	
	Public (N = 54)	Voluntary (N = 22)	Public (N = 158)	Voluntary (N = 153)
	%	%	%	%
No unmet needs reported	61	82	62	76
Unmet needs reported	39	18	38	24
	100	100	100	100

[a] Chi-square = 2.1705; significant at .10 with 1 df.
[b] Chi-square = 6.2613; significant at .023 with 1 df.

No significant differences were demonstrated in three other areas where differences in performance might have been expected to favor the voluntary agencies. For children in 140 families, who were in interim care at the time of the interview, the proportion for whom key decisions still had not been made was virtually the same for both types of agencies: 19 percent for those in public care and 20 percent for those in voluntary agency care. This suggests that the voluntary agencies, again despite their advantages, were no more efficient in determining whether a child should go home or be transferred to long-term care than the public agencies.

For 350 children in some form of institutional care, the proportion reported to be receiving some form of nonroutine attention from the counseling staff was about the same in both types of institutions: 21 percent for the public agencies, 20 percent for those in voluntary care. Of 121 children who had been discharged home at the time of the interview, the proportion reporting some form of followup care was 56 percent for those discharged from the voluntary agencies, only slightly higher than the 51 percent reported for those from the public agencies.

Differences Seen in Substudy Findings

The nature of the substudy, focused as it was on the workers directly, made it possible to compare those who worked in voluntary agencies with those in public agencies in considerably more detail than was possible in the main study.

It was possible to determine from the greater wealth of background detail given in the substudy whether one system recruited its workers from a different population than did the other. The weight of the evidence indicated that they did not, since there were no significant differences in relation to such demographic factors as age, sex, father's occupation, or ethnicity. Neither were there any significant differences in relation to their occupational histories, such as the number of careers considered, the time at which the decision was made to enter social work, undergraduate grades, the influence of friends in the choice of social work, plans for graduate education, or previous social work experience.

Two significant differences, however, suggest that some personality factors may have been operating in the selection of the public or the voluntary sector as an employer. Workers in the voluntary sector were more likely to have reported a desire to work with people as a factor in their selection of social work as a career. They were also significantly more accepting of authority, as measured by the index described in chapter 8, than public agency workers.

Working Conditions

Differences in working conditions between the two sectors generally conform to the picture, obtained from the main study, of a public sector functioning under more stress than the voluntary sector—with one important exception.

Working conditions were reported as poorer by a disproportionately high number of public agency workers. Their case loads were reported as higher and their supervisor turnover as heavier.

Public agency workers experienced significantly more supervisor turnover than voluntary agency workers. A third of the voluntary agency workers enjoyed relative stability—the same supervisor for a period of two years or more—in contrast to only 13 percent of the public agency workers.

TABLE 10.12

Working Conditions and Agency Auspices (N = 222) [a]

	Voluntary (N = 77)	Public (N = 145)
Conditions	%	%
Poor	21	46
Fair	47	42
Good	32	12
	100	100

[a] Chi-square = 19.475; significant under .001 with 1 df.

TABLE 10.13

Caseload Size (Families) and Agency Auspices (N = 131) [a]

	Voluntary (N = 42)	Public (N = 89)
Size	%	%
Less than 20	76	29
20 or more	24	71
	100	100

[a] Chi-square = 23.654; significant under .001 with 1 df.

TABLE 10.14

Supervisor Turnover and Agency Auspices (N = 200) [a]

	Voluntary (N = 73)	Public (N = 127)
Turnover	%	%
At least one change in 2 years or less	67	87
No changes in 2 years	33	13
	100	100

[a] Chi-square = 9.642; significant at .002 with 1 df.

On the other hand, public agency workers earned more than those in the voluntary agencies and also perceived themselves as better off in this respect than their peers.

Nature of Work

Some aspects of the work in the public sector were also different from that of the voluntary agencies. Public agency workers reported a broader age range in their case loads than did voluntary agency workers: 80 percent of the public agency workers said their case loads involved children

TABLE 10.15

Salary in 1966 and Agency Auspices (N = 158) [a,b]

	Voluntary (N = 59)	Public (N = 99)
Salary	%	%
Less than $7000	83	56
Over $7000	17	44
	100	100

[a] Chi-square = 12.001; significance under .001 with 1 df.
[b] Since salary was asked on the questionnaire, only those who responded to it are represented on this table.

TABLE 10.16

Perception of Salary Level and Agency Auspices (N = 205)

	Voluntary (N = 69)	Public (N = 139)
Perceived Salary	%	%
Lower than friends	78	27
Same as friends	19	41
Higher	3	32
	100	100

[a] Chi-square = 52.450; significance under .001 with 2 df.

TABLE 10.17

Procedural Formality and Agency Auspices (N = 214) [a]

	Voluntary (N = 75)	Public (N = 139)
Procedure	%	%
Usually formal	14	28
Mixed	60	58
Usually informal	26	14
	100	100

[a] Chi-square = 8.256; significant at .017 with 2 df.

under the age of two, in contrast to 61 percent of the voluntary agency workers. At the same time, 66 percent of the public agency workers reported case loads including children over 15 in contrast to 40 percent of the voluntary agency workers.

Public agency workers also reported more formality in the procedures used to reach decisions than did voluntary agency workers—i.e. more forms to fill out, staff conferences to attend, etc.

Although they did not differ significantly in assessing the adequacy of their in-service training in general, public agency workers were twice as likely to report that they had felt poorly informed about the nature of their work when they were hired.

Attitudes toward Clients
Although the two groups did not differ significantly from each other with respect to the extent to which they were client- or procedure-oriented,

TABLE 10.18

Agency Auspices and Accuracy of Information (N = 220) [a]

	Voluntary (N = 76)	*Public (N = 144)*
Accuracy of Information	%	%
Poor	20	41
Mixed	31	35
Good	49	24
	100	100

[a] Chi-square = 15.849; significance under .001 with 1 df.

there were a number of more specific questions in which the response showed marked differences. Public agency workers were better able to tolerate client deviance than voluntary agency workers.

TABLE 10.19

Client Deviance and Agency Auspices (N = 220) [a]

	Voluntary (N = 77)	*Public (N = 143)*
Tolerance	%	%
Low	70	54
High	30	46
	100	100

[a] Chi-square = 4.854; significant at the .028 level with 1 df.

Voluntary agency workers were more likely to develop the pattern noted by the interviewers of identifying with either the child or the parent client than were the public agency workers.

Voluntary agency workers were more likely to mention lack of responsiveness and poor case outcome as sources of frustration in their work than were public agency workers. Twenty-two percent of the voluntary agency workers complained of poor case outcome in contrast to 9 percent

TABLE 10.20
Parent-Child Identification and Agency Auspices
(N = 210) [a]

Identification	Voluntary (N = 76) %	Public (N = 134) %
Parent–child	38	17
Equal	62	83
	100	100

[a] Chi-square = 10.373; significant at .002 with 1 df.

of the public agency sample; 18 percent of the voluntary agency sample mentioned lack of responsiveness on the part of clients as a problem in contrast to 8 percent of the public agency workers.

"Pro-Family"
On two questions used in the substudy to measure the extent to which workers identified with the family, both public and voluntary agency workers tended to disagree with the first ("Once a child is placed, it should be up to the family to decide whether it wants help from the agency"), but voluntary agency workers were significantly more likely to disagree "strongly" than the public agency workers. In response to the second statement ("No matter how good a placement may be, most children are better off with their families"), 63 percent of the public agency workers agreed while 59 percent of the voluntary agency workers disagreed.

TABLE 10.21
"Pro-Family" Attitudes and Agency Auspices

Attitudes	"The family should decide . . ." (N = 177) [a]		"No matter how good the placement . . ." (N = 179) [b]	
	Voluntary (N = 66) %	Public (N = 111) %	Voluntary (N = 66) %	Public (N = 113) %
Agree strongly	5	6	15	28
Agree somewhat	18	19	26	35
Disagree somewhat	30	48	32	27
Disagree strongly	47	27	27	10
	100	100	100	100

[a] Chi-square = 8.070; significant at .045 with 3 df.
[b] Chi-square = 12.285; significant at .007 with 3 df.

Satisfactions

When asked to name the sources of satisfaction in their work, most respondents mentioned children (78 percent), a third mentioned families, while 29 percent mentioned the development of their own skills and professional capacities. Agency auspices made no differences with respect to the clients as a source of satisfaction, but public agency workers were significantly more likely to mention their own professional development as a source of satisfaction than did voluntary agency workers.

TABLE 10.22

Casework Skill as a Source of Satisfaction and Agency Auspices
(N = 214) [a]

Skill	Voluntary (N = 76) %	Public (N = 138) %
Not mentioned	80	66
Mentioned	20	34
	100	100

[a] Chi-square = 4.213; significant at .041 with 1 df.

Role Deprivation

On the measure used to assess the worker's sense of role deprivation, public agency workers were more than twice as likely to be among those whose scores were on the deprived end of the scale than the voluntary agency workers.

TABLE 10.23

"Role Deprivation" and Agency Auspices (N = 177) [a]

	Voluntary (N = 65) %	Public (N = 112) %
Not deprived	66	27
Deprived	34	73
	100	100

[a] Chi-square = 24.706; significance under .001 with 1 df.

Value of Work

Consistent with the "role deprivation" pattern is the fact that on the index used to measure the extent to which the workers had positive feelings about the value of the work they did, the majority of the voluntary agency workers had relatively high scores, while the public agency sample was almost evenly divided between high and low scores.

Quality of Service

Public agency workers were much more likely to cite lack of services and facilities for clients as a source of frustration in their work than were voluntary agency workers. They were also much more likely to assess the quality of their own agency's services as poor than were the voluntary agency workers. Workers' feelings that agencies had the "wrong priorities" in their work were also much more prevalent among public agency workers than in voluntary agencies.

TABLE 10.24

"Value of Work" and Agency Auspices (N = 222) [a]

Value	Voluntary (N =77) %	Public (N = 145) %
Relatively low	29	48
Relatively high	71	52
	100	100

[a] Chi-square = 7.255; significant at .008 with 1 df.

TABLE 10.25

Lack of Services as a Source of Frustration and Agency Auspices (N = 216) [a]

	Voluntary (N = 76) %	Public (N = 140) %
Not mentioned	62	42
Mentioned	38	58
	100	100

[a] Chi-square = 6.881; significant at .009 with 1 df.

TABLE 10.26

Worker Opinion of Quality of Services and Agency Auspices (N = 217) [a]

Quality	Voluntary (N = 76) %	Public (N = 141) %
Poor	14	32
Variable	66	63
Good	20	5
	100	100

[a] Chi-square = 16.505; significant under .001 with 2 df.

TABLE 10.27

"Wrong Priorities" and Agency Auspices (N = 216) [a]

Priorities	Voluntary (N = 76) %	Public (N = 140) %
Not mentioned	75	57
Mentioned	25	43
	100	100

[a] Chi-square = 6.023; significant at .015 with 1 df.

Need for Change

Finally, voluntary agency workers were much more likely to be conservative in their assessment of the need for change within the child welfare system as a whole than were public agency workers. The largest group of public agency workers were relatively moderate in their views, as were the voluntary agency workers, but the proportion of "radicals" was more than twice that of the voluntary sample.

TABLE 10.28

Need for Change and Agency Auspices (N = 220) [a]

Need for Change	Voluntary (N = 76) %	Public (N = 144) %
Little	30	17
Some	59	58
High	11	25
	100	100

[a] Chi-square = 9.693; significant at .008 with 2 df.

Summary and Discussion

Comparisons between the public and voluntary agencies involved in the first year of placement indicated that voluntary agencies had the advantage in five areas: lower case loads, more trained and experienced workers, a less problematic case load, less pressure, and fewer complaints about "bureaucratic" obstacles in their work. On the other hand, in relation to those measures which could be seen as a reflection of the quality of work, public agency workers did better than the voluntary agencies on five measures, equally well on three measures, and were weaker on only one.

The substudy findings showed the same pattern of advantages favoring the voluntary system. Although both groups of workers were apparently recruited from the same larger population, the voluntary system appeared to do somewhat better with respect to personality factors. Once in the system, public workers dealt with poorer working conditions, higher case loads, and more supervisor turnover. On the other hand, they were considerably better paid than voluntary agency workers and also perceived themselves to be better off in this regard than their friends.

Public agency workers also evaluated many aspects of their work less favorably than the voluntary agencies: they saw less value in their contacts with other agencies, reported more procedural formality (or more "bureaucracy" as in the main study), and felt poorly informed, at least initially. They were more likely to feel "role deprivation"—i.e., that the tasks they performed were inappropriate—than their voluntary agency counterparts, were less likely to value their work, to feel that service to clients was deficient both qualitatively and quantitatively, and to feel that their agencies assigned the "wrong priorities" in their work; they were also more likely to feel that their administration gave them little support and to feel the need for change more strongly. With respect to clients, however, they were more likely to have a greater tolerance for client deviance, to maintain an equal identification with both parents and children, to be "anti-placement" and "pro-family." They were less likely to complain of poor case outcome. In addition, they were more likely to mention their own professional development as a source of satisfaction than were their counterparts in the voluntary system.

It is also worth noting that on such key measures as the degree of client-orientation and tolerance for ambiguity, the public agency workers did as well as the voluntary agency workers, indicating that they were not themselves more "bureaucratic" in their work orientation, but did perceive the system in which they worked as bureaucratic.

The voluntary system has the advantage, as noted, of lower case loads, better working conditions, and less problematic cases. With these advantages, it would be reasonable to expect more frequent and more intensive contacts with clients, a greater perception of unmet needs, and earlier placement decisions. Yet this does not happen. One can infer either that the relative difference is not large enough to have a consistent impact on worker performance or that power rests so heavily within the public system in the first year that the advantages the voluntary agencies have are of little use and that the resources of better personnel are wasted.

The higher level of discontent among the public workers, together with the same level of client orientation, suggests—as did the data reported in chapter 9—that such discontent is a major force in getting children out of the system and may account for much of the high discharge rate of the first year. Although it is obviously not the only factor, it is clearly a strong one and makes one wonder how many children would leave the system if public agency workers were less critical of it than the evidence here indicates that they are.

chapter eleven

REVIEW AND REFLECTIONS

NINE YEARS DEVOTED to researching a complex agency system resulted in at least two categories of data. One is systematic data—embedded in wall-high shelves of computer output, of which the tables in this report represent a small percentage of the whole and constitute the strongest data in both the statistical and substantive sense. The second category, consisting of unsystematic data, was compiled and processed, in much less orderly fashion, in the mind of the investigator and consists of insights and perceptions derived from formal and informal discussions and the literature, from the perceptions of the workers who were respondents in both studies, and from personal experience. The two categories of data inform one another on occasion, but they sometimes run on parallel tracks and do not meet anywhere. The result is a body of thought on the problems under investigation which is hopefully stimulating and useful to others but does not necessarily constitute a coherent structure.

A rigorous tradition of research reporting usually eliminates or minimizes the second category of data, since it requires the investigator to stay close to his "hard" data and limit his conclusions to those that can be directly documented by the analyses. For this researcher, and for a project as broad in scope and long in time as this one was, the impressions and the reflections produced by the findings are as much a part of the output as the tables, the correlation coefficients, and the statistical tests produced by the computer. They are admittedly secondary to the computer-based findings, though the latter are not so firm and precise as a series of tables makes them appear to be. Direction on what we need to know and do comes from the total experience, not the statistics in isolation. Informed and interested readers will differentiate between documented findings and investigators' interpretations and insights. They will judge the validity of the interpretations and are free to substitute or add their own.

This chapter will recapitulate the key findings, discuss some of their implications, offer some observations about impediments to change, and suggest some further avenues of research.

Key Findings

The effects of agency investment on families and children in foster care were examined through data obtained in telephone interviews with the social workers assigned to 616 children who entered foster care in 1966. Data collection was repeated for a maximum of four cycles over five years. These data were later supplemented by a substudy in which a sample of the workers interviewed in the first year of the original study described and evaluated their work.

The study's principal limitation is that it is a single-role study. It was not possible to examine directly the views of supervisors, foster parents, institutional counselors, or other specialized personnel. The foster care experience from the perspective of the families and the children is reported in the companion volumes to this study. An analysis combining data reflecting all of these perspectives would have been severely limited by the fact that complete matched data at all times would have been available only for a relatively small number of cases as a result of the different patterns of attrition in each sample.

It is likely that the organizational factors would have been more visible had the study been based on a sample of agencies rather than on a sample of children. Nevertheless, the view of children and families as seen by their workers reflects role relations that are central in this system around which everything else revolves.

With these limitations in mind, the following conclusions are presented to summarize the findings reported in the preceding chapters.

1 Over time, families with children in foster care have less contact with agency workers. These contacts are increasingly limited to the mother only and these mothers are increasingly likely to be seen in an unfavorable light, accompanied by decreasing optimism about their ability to make homes for their children. Whatever the problem that precipitates placement, the difficulty encountered by the workers in assessing maternal adequacy is the key reason for continuing placement.

2 Workers perceived the condition of the children they are responsible for as generally good for the first three to four years of placement. After that, the number of children whose emotional state was seen as deteriorating was greater than those seen as improving.

3 Workers question the necessity for placement in relatively few cases. Nevertheless, for those who remained in placement for the full period covered, the experience was seen as damaging to one child in four and to every third or fourth mother.

4 Involvement with other agencies was heavy in the first year only. After that, contact with other agencies declined sharply and the foster care agency dealt with the problems of children and their families in comparative isolation.

5 The longer the children were in care, the more likely they were to be assigned experienced, trained workers with manageable case loads. These more experienced workers, however, were as likely to feel subjective pressure and dissatisfaction with their work as the younger, less experienced workers who were assigned these children in the earlier phases of placement. What satisfactions they experienced were consistently derived from working directly with children, while satisfaction derived from working with families was limited to the first year of placement.

6 The agency's investment—reflected in the form of such assets as worker stability, experience, low case loads, and high frequency of contact—contributed significantly to the discharge rate in the first two years of placement but ceased to be important in the later phases.

7 The workers' evaluation of the mother predicted the child's discharge from care. Unlike all the other variables examined, it contributed significantly to the discharge rate each time. It was superseded in importance only in the third year of placement, when the mother's determination to remove the children from care was stronger than other factors contributing to discharge.

8 The workers' tendency to see improvement in the family is related to some of the service assets described, but not consistently so. Factors associated with the perception of improvement vary at each time and show no stable pattern. Positive evaluations of the mothers predicted improvement at later cycles, suggesting that there is some stability in workers' perceptions of mothers. There was no comparable consistency in their perception of improvement in children.

9 Workers predicted that more children would remain in care than ac-

tually did, suggesting a greater pessimism than is warranted either about the families involved or the system within which they work or their own capacities.

10 Dissatisfaction with client relationships and problems in satisfying the need to give service were a major factor in motivating social workers to try different jobs in fields other than child welfare or enter graduate work to obtain an MSW. Personality patterns such as a tendency to reject authority and an ability to tolerate ambiguity were associated with the achievement of full professionalization, as were strong convictions about the need for social change.

11 Workers' feelings of frustration about the adequacy of the services given and their ability to use informal procedures were associated with early discharge. More than usually frequent contact with clients was associated with the perception of need for change in the system and skepticism about clients' ability to benefit from services.

12 Dissatisfaction with the system was more pronounced in the public sector of the child welfare network than in the voluntary sector.

13 Workers in the voluntary sector had the advantage of working under less pressures. Nevertheless, on a number of performance criteria the public agency's work appeared to be as good, and in some instances better, than that in the voluntary sector.

Implications

No study of this magnitude or complexity would produce findings that imply simply that all is well in the system or that all is a disaster. Some of the implications of the findings can be seen as "good news," followed immediately by other implications that can be viewed as "bad news."

It is good news, for example, that foster care agencies are not simply passive reactors to social conditions beyond their control or to a population of parents with personality disturbances too severe to be treated successfully. If the continuance of children in placement were entirely the result of poverty and lack of opportunity experienced by their parents or of their personal disorganization and immaturity, the variables called service assets would have made little or no difference in the discharge rate. Instead the rate would have been related solely to variables describing the family. That service assets do make a difference within the first two years indicates that agency effort does result in a different picture of the family—one that leads to discharge. By implication, an increase in investment could result in earlier discharges with a reduction in damage for the child, the family, and the public as taxpayers.

On the other hand, it is bad news that the degree of support given by the institution of foster care to families in trouble is very time-limited. The supportive function is fulfilled, if at all, only for about two years after the crisis that precipitates placement. After this, the agency becomes, in effect, a custodian for the child and, as earlier studies have shown, the family is increasingly alienated.

It is "good news" that some factors associated with good casework show some positive results. The recent history of research in social work has been largely that of bad news; a number of studies have presented findings which indicate that casework even under optimum conditions does not produce effective results. Although this study was not focused directly on the quality of the casework involved, it tested some of the basic assumptions related to casework and demonstrated that at least one goal—the return of children in foster care to their families—could be achieved given conditions conducive to good casework. It is especially noteworthy that such successes are achieved largely by BA workers with two to three years of experience.

On the other hand, it is "bad news" that underlying the activism, which leads to discharge, of many of these experienced, committed workers is a strong skepticism about the ability of the system they work in to serve families adequately. Workers seem to become advocates who see themselves trying to protect children from being trapped in a system the workers feel will only damage them. The implications for the system are chilling, to say the least. Were the workers less disenchanted, the "freezing" tendencies of the system would be even stronger than they are and a considerably larger group of children might continue on in care than presently do. If the interests of staff are not to conflict with those of clients, then some motivating power has to be found to replace the drive that is based on disenchantment.

It is good news that the rate of discharge may have improved somewhat in a decade. The Maas and Engler study of foster care pictures a large number of "lost" children solidly entrenched in care with no real effort made to remove them. They noted that "staying in care beyond a year and a half greatly increases a child's chances of growing up in care," [1]

1. Henry S. Maas and Richard Engler, *Children in Need of Parents* (New York: Columbia University Press, 1959), p. 421.

and predicted that "better than half gave promise of living the major part of their childhood years in foster families and institutions." [2] Ten years later, Maas followed up on 88 percent of the original sample of children, placed in the 1950s, and found that 48 percent had left care up to six years after placement. [3] Thus, the figure for this study involving children placed in the mid-1960s, showing one-third still in care after five years, implies some modest improvement.

At the same time, it is bad news that one-third of the children in the sample continued in care, even though this news is not so dismal as might have been anticipated from the earlier research. Like the worker turnover figure of 25 percent, a one-third "residual" of children still in care at the end of five years is not a figure on which the system can congratulate itself, even if it is relatively better than the one produced a decade earlier. Since no service institution can expect total success, what then is a tolerable failure rate? It is very hard to identify a basis on which such an estimate could be made. Perhaps it might be accepted that 10 to 15 percent of the children in care will, by virtue of severe handicaps or complex family situations, spend a childhood in foster homes or institutions, but a rate much higher than this suggests major deficiencies in the services offered.

It is good news that planned permanent foster care may not be so great a necessity as it is deemed to be in some quarters. Influential figures in the child welfare field have recently questioned whether the goal of discharge or adoption for every child is a realistic one. Kline and Overstreet recently wrote that

It has long been a stated and strongly held belief that foster care should not be a way of life for children but rather that it is intended as a short-term treatment measure which, for the children's welfare, must eventuate in their return to their parents or in legal adoption. During the past few years, it has been generally recognized that the experience of foster care agencies does not support this belief. In an important number of cases, these goals are either unattainable or undesirable. [4]

Madison and Schapiro reported a study of the need for long-term foster care in California which

---

2. *Ibid.*, p. 536.
3. Henry S. Maas, "Children in Long-Term Foster Care," *Child Welfare* 48, no. 6, (June 1969): 323.
4. Draza Kline and Helen-Mary Forbush Overstreet, *Foster Care of Children: Nurture and Treatment* (New York: Columbia University Press, 1972), page 51.

learned . . . that long-term foster family care can be a constructive alternative for some children, if it is provided in a purposeful manner and if decisions concerning it are made within a reasonable period of time and in relation to thoroughly considered alternatives. Offered in this way, this type of care reduces anxiety among parents and children alike and frees them to provide satisfying and nurturing relationships with each other.[5]

This need is also seen by these authors as especially pertinent in relation to minority children. At least one large voluntary agency of those who cooperated in this study was a strong advocate of permanent foster care and made it the major part of the service it offered.

Granted that the practice of leaving children in limbo and allowing them to drift is highly undesirable and that no one doubts the importance of early decision-making and planning, there are nevertheless negative aspects to this new emphasis on planned long-term care. A deliberate decision that a child will remain in long-term care until adulthood implies that the worker can predict for a period that may be as long as 18 years that (1) the child's natural family is beyond rehabilitation or change, (2) that the nature of the demand for adoptive children will not change and that a child who was considered hard-to-place in the 1960s will still be hard-to-place in the 1970s, (3) that the larger society is so incapable of change that poor families with few resources today will still be families with few resources a decade later, (4) that the child welfare system's resources will remain limited, so that the services a child will receive in the 1980s will be no better than those of the 1970s.

The atmosphere in American society in the 1970s is conducive to just such pessimism. However, one can still ask—especially after a decade of radical change—whether the particular form of pessimism underlying the promotion of permanent foster care is warranted. In the present study, it was found that workers predicted a return home for fewer children than actually went home more frequently than the reverse error of predicting discharge for those who remained in care. Considering the results obtained from worker effort, one wonders how much more might have been done had the workers been less pessimistic about the future of some of these children. One wonders too whether the rationale for permanent foster care does not mask an underlying need which serves the agency and not the child. A core group of children who are permanently placed relieves the agency of the necessity to reevaluate its goals, in order to

5. Bernice Madison and Michael Schapiro, "New Perspectives on Child Welfare" (San Francisco: Privately printed 1973), p. 163.

respond to changes in the natural family, in the adoption scene, and the community in general. In a system of subsidized voluntary agency care, such as the one examined in this study, a stable group of permanent placements will help assure the financial stability an agency might not otherwise have. Support for planned permanent foster care has in it the quality of a "cop-out." An early decision that a child will require permanent foster care may sometimes be necessary, but the danger of the self-fulfilling prophecy is ever present. In recent years, this has been observed most frequently in the education of minority children in poverty areas: a vicious circle resulting from low expectations in which children are "written off" early as hopeless and are considered not worth the effort involved in teaching them. The need to accept that some children will spend their entire childhood in foster care is analogous to the need to accept that some adults who are physically or mentally ill or retarded will require a lifetime of institutionalization. In both cases, it is clear that these options are last resorts and do not justify the reduction of efforts to achieve less drastic and less damaging solutions.

It is bad news that the time perspective in foster care, at least in the system under scrutiny, is wrong. As was indicated earlier, the administrative standards for this agency network defined three months or less as temporary care. Any longer period was considered long-term care. The data in this study suggest that foster care could be better seen as a two-to four-year experience for those who need it, in which workers concentrate primarily on working toward discharge or adoption while keeping the child in a stable foster home or institutional setting. To set three months as a period in which the child's status is to be established is unrealistically low, considering the complexity of the problems faced by most families. To call any period over three months a long-term placement involves, inappropriately, lumping together those who have a good chance to return home, those who might be adopted, and those who most likely will remain in foster care until adulthood. A change in time perspective to one that is neither too short nor too long may make some goals more achievable and reduce the possibility of drift.

Impediments to Change: Some Observations

On the surface, many changes appear to have taken place in this field during the time covered by the study. If one's information consisted solely of articles in the *New York Times*, one would expect to find a dynamic adaptation to the needs of clients taking place. A review of newspaper reports during this period describes many seemingly significant changes. A whole series of innovations designed to open up adoption services is described: subsidies, relaxed standards, preference to foster parents, single-parent adoption, interracial adoption, adoption by families with biological children, adoption of handicapped and older children, and a new adoption agency in the black community. Legislation on behalf of abused children, a reporting system, and new services for the abuséd are also described. So are the closing of inadequate institutions, the replacement of shelters by group care, and the building of new facilities. The availability of funds for services to children in their own homes is reported. Legislation to clarify procedures for the termination of parental rights has been introduced. Recruitment efforts for foster parents and establishment of the rights of foster parents to appeal agency decisions are also described.

Parallel to these reported changes, however, one finds in the press repeated attacks on the foster care network for the overcrowding and inadequacy of its shelters, for its inability to serve older children in need of supervision, for breakdowns in interagency communication, for disorganization and ineffectiveness in the courts, for failure to provide funds for preventive care or to use them when allocated, for the selectivity and inadequacies of the voluntary agency system, and for the high cost of foster care.

Some of the improvements seem to be direct responses to these criticisms, but experienced observers know that many of these signs of change cannot be interpreted literally. Plans are announced and dropped as obstacles arise, new services turn out to be less useful than was expected, changes in policy are sabotaged subtly or otherwise by staff who cannot accept change. Which of the heralded changes are genuine and which are not would be a major study in itself. To this observer, the changes appear for the most part to be relatively limited, easing some situations for some clients and assuring something better for others. In general, however, one has a sense of a basic conservatism which must yield to major external pressures before any inroads are made. Most critics of the system were saying many of the same things in 1973 when this study was completed that they were in 1966 when it began. Why then should a system of services of which there is much criticism by the press and the interested public and so much internal discontent be so incapable of basic change?

There are no doubt many explanations, but at least two are relevant here. One of them lies in the structure of the system and the other in its ideology. To understand the structural problem, recall that the findings indicated that worker experience is misplaced in this system. The voluntary agencies have a relatively large group of experienced, trained workers but, since intake is largely the function of the public agency, they are usually not involved with the children in care and their families until the second year of placement or later. Yet worker experience contributes to discharge in the first year of placement. It follows then that the more experienced workers should be involved in the first year of placement, not later. This simply confirms a long acknowledged principle of practice that a high level of worker experience should be invested in intake. To follow through on this finding would require a shift in manpower from the voluntary system to the public system, which only a strong public system could enforce, or it would require the complete takeover of intake procedures by the voluntary agencies, as they have in fact recommended.[6] The latter move, however, would weaken the accountability structure even further.

Structural Difficulties

The weaknesses in the current system of accountability are described by Levitt in his dissertation, and the essential points may be recapitulated as follows. In 1964, shortly before this study was begun, the voluntary agencies participated in the redrafting of the "Rules and Recommendations for Child-caring Institutions" of the State Board of Child Welfare and were given "guarantees of managerial autonomy and freedom to pursue sectarian objectives. [The voluntary agencies] . . . were deemed to be the sole judge of the suitability of their services and could therefore completely control their intake." [7] Attempts made later to set up a more effective accountability system were resisted by the agencies, and eventually the State Board found

that there are no agreements or contracts currently between the Bureau of Child Welfare and the large number of . . . voluntary agencies from which it purchases foster care for children. This means that there are no specific agreements as to the extent of responsibility of either the public agency or the voluntary agencies in the child field. . . .

6. Louis Levitt, *The Accountability Gap in Foster Care: Discontinuities in Accountability in the Purchase and Provision of Foster Care Services in New York City* (PhD diss., Graduate School of Public Administration, New York University, 1972), p. 168.

7. *Ibid.*, page 76.

The 1967 understanding put the Department in the position of rubber-stamping most voluntary agency decisions and did not provide BCW staff with effective instruments for oversight of care purchased from voluntary agencies. The most important set of issues both with respect to their fiscal consequences and the needs of service recipients was the lack of control over decisions by voluntary agencies regarding continuity of casework with natural parents. [8]

Since pressures within the long-term care agency to work with parents are negligible, accountability is particularly important in this area and it is precisely here that it is lacking. As Levitt states:

Continuing contact with natural parents is subject to the judgment of each agency within a weak accountability structure based on the agency's own written reports, which cannot help but be self-serving. Maintenance of contact with natural parents is bound to require a costly investment of staff time. . . . The reimbursement system based upon a fixed per diem rate for child care does not make any extra allowance for extra expense involved in such contacts. Agencies are paid a fixed amount, no matter whether contact is maintained or not. The rate simply assumes that responsibility for contact has been delegated to the agency and the agency is presumed to be ready, willing, and able to make the necessary investment. . . . Without a radical shift from present policy towards an effective accountability structure, the rate increase indicates no sound basis for increased work with natural parents in order to return children to their homes. The reimbursement structure asks agencies to invest time and therefore funds in disrupting a presumably stable living arrangement to return the child home and therefore conceivably end reimbursement until the vacancy can be filled. . . . When the vacancy is filled, an additional investment of staff time is necessary in order to reach a level of stability. . . . Agencies therefore are being asked to work against their managerial interests to perform a service for which they will be paid even if the service is not performed. . . . The compulsion under which they labor is composed of equal parts of a professional "spirit of craftsmanship" and law and regulations so riddled with escape clauses as to be ineffective. [9]

Levitt documents further the absence of appeal procedures and fair hearing mechanisms as well as the intimidating language of the voluntary commitment form, all of which contributes to keeping the natural family at a distance.

The weak accountability structure may be charged to the nature of political power in New York of which the sectarian-affiliated voluntary

8. *Ibid.*, pp. 91, 93. As this manuscript is being prepared for publication a new contract has been written which is purported to be comparatively strong. Its impact, of course, remains to be seen.
9. *Ibid.*, page 135.

agencies are a part. The influence of these powers may be more keenly felt in New York than elsewhere but as Levitt notes:

The problem of prolonged foster care is endemic in child welfare nationally. The whole system is balanced in favor of agency decision-making in the absence of effective weighting and communication of client concerns. Like many governmental systems, foster care does best by simply continuing since the extra effort involved in planning and implementing termination is outside the system's present behavioral norms.[10]

Levitt notes that a policy of reimbursement to agencies for expenses incurred in connection with the discharge of children in care was introduced in 1971, as was a policy of reimbursement for expenses in connection with adoption; their effectiveness remains to be demonstrated. Later, a law requiring a court review of placement decisions was passed. Agencies must now demonstrate continuous planning for children and justify their decisions to the court every two years, but this law is now in the process of being implemented and its effectiveness remains to be demonstrated. The voluntary agencies have made their case [11] on the basis of long experience, a high level of professional skill, and the need to defend the religious interests of their clients. Whatever the merits of their position, it does not alter the fact that a partnership as weak as this one is very limited in its ability to function effectively in meeting the needs of its clients.

Ideological Difficulties
The relationship between the belief system and the problem of change in social agency practice is subtler and even harder to demonstrate than the problems of developing a system of accountability. That there is a strong belief that the goal of foster care should be the reunion of children with their families is readily documented in the literature and has provided the basic assumption on which the analysis of the study's findings was based. The findings here have indicated, as have other studies before it, that this belief is more honored than real.

The prolongation of care may be reinforced by the fact that there is yet another sacred belief in the child welfare system which is not altogether compatible with belief in the importance of keeping families together.

10. *Ibid.*, page 158.
11. Monsignor Robert Arpie, Thomas A. DeStefano, Dr. Edward Hawthorne, Jacob Trobe, *Voluntary Child Care in New York City*, 1974 (New York: privately printed).

This belief is expressed in the high priority given to the maintenance of children in stable situations for as long as possible with a corollary view of change as inevitable traumatic and damaging. That the system does not succeed in insuring stability any more than it succeeds in reuniting families is seen in the fact that, of the children in care for the full five-year span of the study, only 18 percent had a single placement. The average number of placements for the sample was 2.4.[12] Part of this instability is based on the way the system is structured—with its use of temporary shelters or boarding homes before the decision for long-term care—but this is not the only reason for replacement. Fully 42 percent of the children in the study had more than the two placements, usually imposed by the system. Shinn's analysis of replacement patterns indicated that most were for negative reasons. They were most likely to be the result of unsuitable foster home placements or problems in the foster family or agency requirements (religious matching, age limitations, program closings, etc.). Few changes came about because of anticipated benefits to the child.[13]

Even so, the value attached to stability can be used as a rationale for maintaining the children in the system as opposed to returning the child to his own home or releasing him for adoption. As evidence that the value attached to stability can be seen as superseding all others, consider the following statement by Kline and Overstreet:

Legal adoption by another family is contra-indicated for some children who are well integrated emotionally into a stable foster home at the time the parents' legal rights are terminated. . . . when the foster family provides good care and wants the child permanently, the damage that results from transfer to another family to effect a legal adoption may outweight any potential advantage.[14]

Elsewhere the same authors speak of the need to maintain an equilibrium or balance between the foster child, his parents, and the agency. Illustrations of good casework given in the same text focus on situations in which overburdened foster mothers are supported through a crisis in which the resolution is the continuation of the child in the home. In and of themselves these principles are laudatory, but in the context of the

12. Eugene B. Shinn, "Placement Patterns: A Five-Year Analysis of Placement, Replacement and Discharge of CWRP Study Children," Child Welfare Research Program, xeroxed (New York: Columbia University School of Social Work), p. 20.
13. *Ibid.*, pp. 25–26.   14. Kline and Overstreet, *Foster Care*, p. 56.

present discussion the constant emphasis on the supportive functions of the worker in maintaining the foster-parent–child relationships makes so drastic a change as a return to the natural parent or a movement toward adoption seem too much of a disruption and risk. Especially for the child who has been in care two years or more, enough agencies and workers must be willing to take such risks if the freezing process inherent in the foster care situation is to be contained.

It is worth noting, parenthetically, that nowhere in the text cited is there a reference to the economic implications of decisions to support permanent foster care placements. It is implicit in the discussions of many leading figures in the field—particularly among those whose training and experience is in casework—that the profession must support whatever it deems best for clients, regardless of the consequences for the taxpayer. It is assumed that if the desired service is an expensive one that the funds, private or public, must be found for it. This is again a valid position in many ways, but those who take it must acknowledge that the cost of a program, in these days of heavy competitive demands on the welfare budget, is not a minor consideration. The more costly a social program, the greater the obligation of the concerned professional to justify its use to the public. The high cost of permanent foster care has been demonstrated in another study emanating from this project.[15] The need to continue children in foster care seemed unavoidable to most of the workers in this study, but one wonders what might have happened had the pressure to justify such placements been greater.

Another unintended and relatively unnoticed consequence of the emphasis on stability is the measure of control it gives the foster parents over the child's situation, with which the agency is relatively powerless to deal if it subscribes fully to the primacy of maintaining stability. Even with the advantage of a subsidy program, foster parents can legitimately refuse to adopt for whatever reasons they may have. If the child seems secure in the home and workers accept the high premium placed on stability, which negates plans to move a child solely for the purpose of adoption, the only alternative is to maintain the status quo. Foster parents are relatively underrewarded and have little legal power over the children they care for, but the power to provide stability is theirs at the same time that demands for full legal and economic responsibility are not made on

15. David Fanshel and Eugene B. Shinn, *Dollars and Sense in the Foster Care of Children* (New York: Child Welfare League of America, 1972).

them. Valued foster parents apparently can have considerable bargaining power with their agencies. The latter are then reinforced in their own administrative interests in maintaining stability and are virtually impelled to find an ideological justification for permanent foster care.

Whether foster parents, however sound their motivations, can really give total emotional security to a child without taking on the full responsibility of parenthood is an open question. The presence of an agency provides the foster parents with an escape that neither natural nor adoptive parents have. A child must inevitably be aware that, no matter how stable the foster home placement may be, his foster parents have a less-than-full commitment to him.

Thus the administrative need to maintain the status quo is inadvertently reinforced by a value system which places the highest priority on stability. The very fact that changes which the agencies cannot control are often forced on the children may only reinforce the need to maintain what stability there is—which in turn leads again to resistance to the more drastic decisions of return home or adoption.

The arguments for permanent foster home care have received some reinforcement in some of the principles promulgated in the recent widely publicized *Beyond the Best Interests of the Child*. One of these is the principle that "placements should provide the least detrimental available alternative for safeguarding the child's growth and development." [16] This guideline reinforces two others laid down by the authors: "Placement decisions should safeguard the child's need for continuity of relationships," and "should reflect the child's not the adult's sense of time." [17]

The authors justify the concept of "least detrimental alternatives" on the grounds that

To use "detrimental" rather than "best interest" should enable legislatures, courts, and child care agencies to acknowledge and respond to the inherent detriments in any procedure for child placement as well as in each child placement decision itself. It should serve to remind decisionmakers that their task is to salvage as much as possible out of an unsatisfactory situation. It should reduce the likelihood of their becoming enmeshed in the hope and magic associated with "best" which often mistakenly leads them into believing that they have greater power for doing "good" than "bad." [18]

16. Joseph Goldstein, Anna Freud, Albert Solnit, *Beyond the Best Interests of the Child* (New York: The Free Press, 1973), p. 53.
17. *Ibid.*, pp. 31, 40.   18. *Ibid.*, pp. 62–63.

While a persuasive case can be made for all of these principles, at least one critic has pointed out that they can justify non-intervention in the lives of children not involved in custody suits or in danger of physical harm, and could be used by conservative forces to rationalize passivity, especially in the current atmosphere of disillusionment.[19]

It must be noted, however, that the frame of reference of *Beyond the Best Interests* is legal, and the major content of the discussion is drawn from custody suits in which there are two contending parents. For the child in "permanent" foster care, the alternative to the marginal foster parent or the one reluctant to adopt is an adoptive home to be located by the agency. Dr. Solnit, in replying to the criticism noted, indicated that the principle in question had been intended to limit the tendency to look for "perfection" in placement decisions.[20] One can question whether a search for an adoptive home can be equated with a search for "perfection." The question foster care agencies must ask is whether the imperfect but familiar foster home, which cannot or will not offer permanence, is indeeed better than the unfamiliar, imperfect adoptive home which does.

Perhaps the most basic change needed in the long run is a replacement of the present pattern of differentiating services between natural, adoptive, and foster homes. Services for natural parents have been available largely at times of crisis. Services for adoptive parents have been limited to the application and placement periods and terminated with legal adoption. The foster home relationship, by contrast, has been an indeterminate one in which the agency gives full support as long as the foster parents want to continue in that role and are able to do so. With the decline of infant placement and increasing emphasis on the placement of older children, particularly those with emotional and physical handicaps, these patterns may need to be replaced by one in which the agency assumes full financial responsibility for the child only in the transition phase to the foster or adoptive family and provides supportive services, including counseling and financial aid, for as long as any of the families in question need it. Most of the basic problems of child-rearing are common to all families; once the child's status is permanent, the category labels of natural, adoptive, or foster may be more artificial than real. The

19. The Honorable Justine Polier in an address before the meeting of the American Association of Psychiatric Services for Children, New York City, November 23, 1974.
20. Response to Judge Polier's address at the same meeting.

underlying need for support in the process of parenting is common to all of them.

Such a radical change in practice would require basic changes in the laws that govern child placement. Legal recognition of the status of "psychological parent" proposed by the authors of *Beyond the Best Interests* is perhaps its strongest and most constructive point. Their model child placement statute defines the psychological parent as follows:

A psychological parent is one who, on a continuing, day-to-day basis, through interaction, companionship, interplay, and mutuality, fulfills the child's psychological needs for a parent, as well as the child's physical needs. The psychological parent may be a biological . . . adoptive, foster or common-law parent, or any other person. There is no presumption in favor of any of these after the initial assignment at birth.[21]

Recognition of such a status would in effect direct agencies to support the adults who fulfill the definition most satisfactorily. Precedence would not necessarily be given to biological parents, as it is under present law.

Equal recognition for the status of parent, regardless of its origins, would also underscore the inequities of the present system in which financial aid to natural parents (AFDC) is considerably less than either foster home payments or subsidies to adoptive parents. A system in which the parent minimally capable of rearing children is supported in his or her role by the social service network or relieved of the parenting role if clearly incapable is certainly preferable to the present system, filled as it is with contradictions and inequities.

Some Further Observations

On the Question of Race

The informed reader, aware of the role played by the problems of race and ethnicity in contemporary American social problems, will note that these have not entered heavily into the presentation of the findings of this study. Findings reported in chapters 3 and 7 indicated that black and Puerto Rican children have greater difficulty in leaving the system than do white children, most of whom have left by the third year of placement. Another finding in chapter 9 indicated that black workers were more likely to remain with their agencies than white workers. As was sug-

21. Goldstein, Freud, Solnit, *Beyond the Best Interest*, p. 98.

gested, this may occur because black workers take longer to achieve these positions and have less security about the choices available to them. On the other hand, it also implies a greater potential for power within the system for black staff.

The fact that there are relatively few statistically significant differences related to race does not reflect lack of awareness on the part of the investigators. The influence of the race of the child, the mother, and the workers was examined in every analysis. That there are significant attitudinal differences between white, Puerto Rican, and black families in this sample was demonstrated by Jenkins and Norman in their studies of the natural families. Differences in the children by ethnicity were discerned by Fanshel and Shinn.[22] But none of these differences in the client group are reflected in the agency phase of the study. A white mother, whose child was not in a residential treatment center, did not necessarily get a better trained or more experienced worker than did a black or a Puerto Rican mother. Nor did a worker necessarily evaluate a white mother in more positive terms than she did a black or Puerto Rican mother. Nor was a white child necessarily seen as more appealing. This was consistent with findings of the substudy, which suggested that workers were not particularly aware of or sensitive to subcultural differences.

These negative findings indicate that individuals working in the system are relatively free of bias, but it does not mean that the structure of the system as a whole works in favor of minority groups. The picture that emerges from this study is one in which a relatively small group of children—those placed for emotional disturbance who are usually white and Jewish—received an adequate and appropriate service in this network of agencies. They were treated intensively in settings with high professional standards for a period of two or three years, at the end of which they were discharged to their families in an improved condition—at least in the eyes of their workers. They seldom needed temporary shelter care and the question of adoption rarely arose. All other children, usually black or Puerto Rican, whose emotional problems were overshadowed by the more visible disturbances of their parents, shared equally in the deficiencies and inadequacies of the system. It could be argued that given the greater social disadvantages suffered by these children before they came

---

22. Shirley Jenkins and Elaine Norman, *Filial Deprivation and Foster Care* (New York: Columbia University Press, 1972), ch. 5; David Fanshel and Eugene B. Shinn, *Children in Foster Care* (New York: Columbia Uncversity Press, in process).

into the foster care network, they should have received a heavier investment of service. Instead, the quality of service they received was more a matter of chance than of any planned or rationally thought out program.

For the Future

Since research is, or should be, a continuing enterprise, a concluding word must be devoted to future lines of research. Out of this study, at least two main lines are suggested. During the period covered here, the agency network involved established a computerized system of data collection on all of its clients which, at this writing, is in the early stages of implementation. At present, the data it collects describe the child, its family, and the plans made. With the addition of a few salient variables about the services given, it should be possible to test the relationship between services and discharge or other forms of change and to test the effectiveness of innovations. In fact, had a computerized data collection system been introduced in the child welfare field when this study was planned, the expense of obtaining the data in a series of field operations would not have been necessary.

Studies based on information systems would produce more soundly based conclusions because of the large sample sizes possible, but this is no substitute for new studies which pursue the questions raised by this one in greater depth. This study has demonstarated that the workers' evaluation of the mother is central for the movement of children out of the system and that the workers' difficulties in assessing maternal adequacy are a major factor in keeping children in placement. What enters into that evaluation? It was not possible in this study to probe this question in any greater depth than was indicated in chapter 7. The general impression derived from the interview material is that the criteria are vague and idiosyncratic. It is more likely that there is an agency subculture of beliefs and attitudes, influenced by some of the pressures we have discussed, which controls the evaluations made. Clarification of what underlies worker assessments of adequate mothering should have some impact on bringing the foster care system closer to the goal of functioning as a truly supportive system for the family.

INDEX

Administrative support: index measure, 148–49; optimism about discharge, 168

Age: of study children, 44; of workers, 159

Agencies: atmosphere, 106, 138–39; auspices, 109; hierarchy, 139; involvement with families, 61–63; participation in main study, 17–18; policy, 139; procedural formality, 186; professional attention, 63; professionalism of staff, 136–37; public assistance, 62; structural difficulties, 203–5; unmet needs, 63

"Anti-elitism": scale, 147–48; and training, 155

Arpie, R., 205n.

Attitudes of workers: and discharge of children, 160–64; impact on clients, 161–69

Authority: index measure, 142–43; and training, 154

Beyond the Best Interests of the Child, 208–9

Bieri, J., 143n.

Billingsley, A., 128, 146n.

Blau, P., 126–27

Budner, S., 144n.

Bureaucratic procedures, and agency auspices, 178

Bureau of Child Welfare, 9, 18

Career decisions: and contact with children, 167; timing of, 146, 155–56

Caseload: 7, 89–90; and agency auspices, 184–85; and discharge, 79–81; and improvement in child, 84; and improvement in mother, 88; in public and voluntary agencies, 176–77; in substudy, 139–40

Catholic agencies, 99–100

Change: ideological obstacles to, 205–10; impediments to, 201–3

"Child appeal," 48–50, 108

Child sample: age of, 44; educational problems of, 47–48; emotional problems of, 46–47; ethnicity of, 45; health of, 45–56; intelligence of, 46; religion of, 45; sex of, 44; siblings of, 29–30; socioeconomic status of, 45, and effect on improvement in family, 106; wedlock status of, 45

Child Welfare Research and Demonstration Grants Program, viii, 3

Child Welfare Research Program, viii–ix, 2–3

PUBLICATIONS OF THE CHILD WELFARE
AND FAMILY WELFARE RESEARCH PROGRAM

Borgatta, Edgar F., and David Fanshel. "The Child Behavior Characteristics (CBC) Form: Revised Age-Specific Forms." *Multivariate Behavioral Research*, 5 (January 1970), 49–81.

Fanshel, David. "The Exit of Children from Foster Care: An Interim Research Report." *Child Welfare*, 50 (February 1971), 65–81.

——— "Parental Failure and Consequences for Children: The Drug Abusing Mother Whose Children Are in Foster Care." *American Journal of Public Health* (June 1974), 604–12.

——— "Parental Visiting of Children in Foster Care: Key to Discharge?" *Social Service Review*, 4 (forthcoming, December 1975).

——— "Status Changes of Children in Foster Care: Final Results of the Columbia University Longitudinal Study." *Child Welfare*, 55 (forthcoming, March 1976).

Fanshel, David, and Eugene B. Shinn. *Children in Foster Care: A Longitudinal Investigation*. New York: Columbia University Press (forthcoming).

——— *Dollars and Sense in the Foster Care of Children*. New York: Child Welfare League of America, 1972 (47 pages).

Jenkins, Shirley. "Filial Deprivation in Parents of Children in Foster Care." *Children*, 14 (January–February 1967), 8–12.

——— "Separation Experiences of Parents Whose Children Are in Foster Care." *Child Welfare*, 48 (June 1969), 334–40.

Jenkins, Shirley, and Elaine Norman. *Beyond Placement: Mothers View Foster Care*. New York: Columbia University Press, 1975 (152 pages).

——— "Families of Children in Foster Care." *Children*, 16 (July–August 1969), 155–59.

——— *Filial Deprivation and Foster Care*. New York: Columbia University Press, 1972 (296 pages).

Norman, Elaine. "Some Correlates of Behavioral Expectations: A Role Study of Mothers with Children in Foster Care Placement." Unpublished Ph.D. dissertation, City University of New York, 1972 (204 pages).

Shapiro, Deborah. "Agency Investment in Foster Care: A Follow-Up." *Social Work*, 18 (November 1973), 3–9.

——— "Agency Investment in Foster Care: A Study." *Social Work*, 17 (July 1972), 20–28.

———— "Occupational Mobility and Child Welfare Workers: An Exploratory Study." *Child Welfare*, 53 (January 1974), 5–13.

———— "Professional Education and the Child Welfare Worker: An Exploratory Study," in *Approaches to Innovation in Social Work Education*. New York: Council on Social Work Education, 1974; pp. 82–91.